WHAT FAUST THE DANCING CAT TAUGHT ME

Signe A. Dayhoff, PhD

What Faust the Dancing Cat Taught Me
By Signe A. Dayhoff, PhD

Copyright © 2015 by Signe A. Dayhoff, PhD
Published by Effectiveness-Plus Publications LLC
80 Paseo de San Antonio
Placitas, New Mexico 87043-8735

Photo of gray cat with permission from Fotosearch.com

All rights reserved

ISBN: 978-0-9671265-5-5

No part of this book may be reproduced, stored in a retrieval system, or transmitted in any form or by any means, electronic, mechanical photocopying, microfilming, recording, or otherwise, without written permission from the author, except for the inclusion of brief quotations in a review.

Disclaimer: This publication is designed to provide accurate information in regard to the subject matter covered. It is sold with the understanding that the publisher is not engaged in rendering psychological or any other professional service. The instruction, ideas, and advice are not intended as a substitute for medical or psychological counseling. The reader should consult a professional to determine the nature of their problem and if expert assistance is needed, they should seek the services of a competent professional. The author and publisher disclaim any responsibility or liability resulting from application of procedures presented or discussed in this book.

DEDICATION

This memoir is dedicated to all who have ever had a cat companion, to those who rescue cats (especially Dr. Barbara Bayer, president of the all-volunteer, non-profit Companion Animal Rescue and Medical Assistance in Corrales, New Mexico, who creates rescue, treatment, and adoption miracles and from whom most of my fur kids came), and to those who have not as yet experienced the overwhelming physical, psychological, and spiritual joy of having and loving a cat.

To Dr. Jeffrey Katuna of Wellesley-Natick Veterinary Hospital, 359 Worcester Road, Natick, for skillfully having set Faust on the road to health and happiness.

This is also dedicated to all my feline companions over the decades, whom I remember with sweetest memories, who have gone over the Rainbow Bridge … and to those individuals still with me who fill my daily life with love and litter. They are, in alphabetical order: Angel, Bailey, Barnaby, Boggs, Buddy, Buster, Carmella, Cramer, Dobby, Donovan, Foxy, George, Groucho, Kiri, Lucky, Maxie, Paula, Phoenix, Pyewacket, Rambo, Sherman, Smoochie, Squeaky, Sweetums, and Trinity.

TABLE OF CONTENTS

1. STARTING A NEW LIFE 1
2. BEING OWNED BY A CAT 11
3. WORKING TOGETHER 26
4. VISITING THE VET 35
5. PILLING FOR FUN AND PROFIT 43
6. LEAVING HIM ALONE 53
7. GOING OUT 61
8. MINDING HIS ETIQUETTE 73
9. VIEWING PREFERENCES 81
10. CONSTRUCTING A CAT TREE 86
11. DOING ROCKPORT 93
12. EXERCISING WITH MOM 103
13. EXPANDING HIS REPERTOIRE 110
14. TRIPPING THE LIGHT FANTASTIC 117
15. TRICKING OR TREATING 121
16. MEETING WINTER HEAD ON 126
17. SINGING 'TIS THE SEASON 130
18. DRIVING TO FLORIDA 141
19. ENCOUNTERING A REDNECK COP 152
20. TAKING TO THE AIR 158
21. PLAYING THE HAMMERED DULCIMER . 165
22. NAVIGATING HOME 180
23. WHAT FAUST TAUGHT ME 190
ABOUT THE AUTHOR 195

ACKNOWLEDGMENTS

No book becomes a practical reality without the encouragement of others. So to all who urged me to start writing about my fabulous adventures with Faust, I offer my whole-hearted thank you for this. I have been privileged to have the assistance of numbers of people, including Judith Sherven PhD and Jim Sniechowski PhD, *New York Times* bestselling authors and executive coaches, who read an early draft and made important suggestions. I offer my undying gratitude to the many dozens of human cat-companions who shared with me their own unique, and often hilariously funny, cat stories as well as their identification with Faust's tales. But most of all, I thank Faust for finding me in the first place when I really needed him, being the eccentric, talented, loving, and inspiring feline he was, and making me a better, more understanding human being as a result of knowing him as a cat companion and alter ego.

CHAPTER 1

STARTING A NEW LIFE
✹✹

As far back as I can remember, I always had a rescue cat which I loved and protected ... and which loved me back as no one else did. This was a warm, wonderful relationship that defied description. It was the only stability in my young life within my emotionally and behaviorally dysfunctional family. We were frequently on the move because of my father's undiagnosed bipolar impairment, from his grandiose highs to his depressive lows, his resulting intermittent unemployment, and our inability to pay the rent.

When my family had to move the last time in order for us to mooch off relatives, my beloved cat, Sam, was "given away" to strangers. That meant my cat could no longer count on me to always be there for him. And he could no longer share himself and his love with me. I worried that anyone else would or could love him as much as I did, would give him as much attention and care as I did. As a result, I was left with a gnawing sense of my loss and connection and his abandonment.

Because of my lingering pain and mismanaged emotions about seemingly "dumping" Sam, I was less willing to involve myself in that kind of companion-animal relationship ever again—and especially in that special love bond (that only a cat companion can provide). That is, *unless* I could unequivocally guarantee I would always be there for the cat, to care for and love it, never leave it, much less "give it away," no matter what. No, I absolutely could never—would never—abandon my beloved cat—my trusted and trusting friend, life-companion, antic playmate, and confidante—ever again.

After finally extricating myself from my mentally unbalanced family situation, I went to college and graduate school, working nights and weekends so I was rarely at home. Then in 1976 I moved to the small town of Sudbury, Massachusetts. Sudbury, which was named after the town of that name in the East Anglia region, in Suffolk, in eastern England, is a beautiful tree-enshrouded, rural community west of Boston. It's situated on Route 20, better known as Boston Post Road.

At one time Sudbury covered forty square miles, encompassing also Wayland and Maynard and was purchased from local Native Americans, perhaps of the Cato or

Cutshamakin tribes. Now it covers only a little more than twenty-four square miles. The first permanent Colonial settlement of about one hundred-thirty men, women, and children was in 1638. It was then founded in 1639.

It boasts a long and prestigious history. Among other things, the townspeople held off Native American King Philip and his band in King Philip's War in 1675. Longfellow's Wayside Inn, the oldest operating Inn in the country, resides there. It has offered comfort and hospitality to travelers along the Boston Post Road since 1716. Furthermore, in 1775 militia and Minutemen from Sudbury fought in the Revolutionary War not only at Lexington and Concord but also later at Bunker Hill, Ticonderoga, Saratoga, and White Plains. In addition, residents of Sudbury have long valued the town for its beauty, fertile ground for growing produce, access to the tranquil Sudbury River, and its abundance of wildlife and wetlands for migrating birds.

It was in these inviting surroundings that I rented a small two-level house with silver-green-stained vertical wood siding, with a single-car garage, in a quiet, tree-strewn neighborhood. From there I would continue my communications business, which I had started the year before in Nahant. Nahant is a small resort town of rocky coasts on a peninsula in

Massachusetts Bay, connected to the city of Lynn by a causeway. There I did a variety of freelance writing, such as marketing, advertising, and white papers, and editing projects, such as technical articles and fiction manuscripts.

I had been luxuriating in Sudbury for only three months when I volunteered to give a speech at the Goodnow Library on the history of the Equal Rights Amendment. This was a project on which I had been working passionately for several years. Goodnow is a public library of which Benjamin Franklin, who created the subscription library system in 1730, would have been proud. The community event at which I was to speak was scheduled for seven o'clock in the meeting room on the first floor of the library on Concord Road, just off Rt. 20. Little did I know the full impact and consequences of my presentation that evening.

I parked my avocado green VW Rabbit in behind the two-story brick building on the graveled space hung low with maple tree and sycamore boughs. Making my way around to the front, I was gratified to see that we had a packed hall. There would be other presentations to explain precisely what the amendment stated and actually implied, contrary to what some of the alarm-raising dissenters claimed, creating a great deal of confusion.

Considering how many public and private bathrooms were already "unisex" by practicality, for example, I couldn't understand how people would accept the bathroom excuse as a reason not to pass this justice amendment. But this was not my first foray into politics and the political spin used to create immediate negative emotional impact. Spin, I had found, was generally used to engender fear in those who had no idea what the proposed amendment really said.

Settling in at the podium, I explained that the ERA was a simple justice amendment which was first proposed in 1923 to affirm that women and men should have equal rights under the law. Perfectly reasonable to my way of thinking. However, those who wanted to maintain the status quo of men having more rights than women did, with what that meant for pay and attendant power, disagreed. Despite its 1923 origin, it was not until 1972 that the ERA was passed out of Congress.

It was ultimately ratified by thirty-five states, but still needed a total of thirty-eight states in order to become the 28th Amendment to the Constitution. Just three more states. While Massachusetts had ratified the amendment, there was still some confusion about its content and implementation. Those states which had not yet ratified it existed primarily in the South and Southwest.

Just as I was finishing my opening statement, something small, gray and white, toothsome, and shabby stuck its head around the door jamb to the meeting room for only a second. It stopped me. It was some kind of animal but I couldn't tell what it was from my brief look. I wanted to call, "Come on in," but didn't. The unknown animal peeked in several more times during my speech. Then it seemed to disappear into the rapidly-oncoming darkness. I smiled to myself.

One of the things I liked about living in a rural setting was that animals of all kinds, from raccoons to deer, might wander into your yard and, if you weren't careful, into your house. That generally created panic for both humans and animals so you had to be mindful about open garages or unlocked doors, and garbage.

When the meeting ended at 8:45 p.m., there was an enjoyably vigorous question-and-answer session. Some participants armed with misinformation wanted to argue and emotionally disregard the facts. But, for the most part, people simply wanted to be fully informed and asked reasonable questions. In return they received reasonable, straightforward answers.

Pleased we may have contributed something worthwhile to those assembled, I walked back to my car. My mind was filled with articles I wanted to submit to the local papers as well as the *Boston Globe* and *Boston Herald* on what we had covered in the meeting, the public's response to it, and why it was still important.

Pre-occupied, I was oblivious to my surroundings. At first I didn't see my small speech intruder. But as I approached the back of my car, I spotted something in the pearlescent gray of the rapidly-oncoming summer twilight. It was huddled just under the car by my right rear tire. Something like a squirrel, but, then again, nothing like one. It wasn't until I was three feet away that it raised its pointy-earred head. I couldn't believe it. It was a cat. But given its incredibly gaunt appearance, it was more like the shadow of a former-cat

It rose to greet me on wobbly legs. Now I saw its prominent ribs, hips, and skull. My stomach knotted. My nose reddened. My eyes began to fill with tears. I wondered how much longer this small sad creature would have left to live.

Even in the dim light emanating from the meeting room windows, I could see the insides of its ears were dark brown with coffee-grounds-like detritus. This was undoubtedly blood from ravaging ear mites. It wheezed as it hobbled toward me to wrap its bony tail around my legs. I had seen homeless people on the streets of sections of

Boston, living in cardboard hovels and on subway grates, in better shape than this.

It raised its skin-stretched head to look at me. Its deep amber eyes glinted with a fire that hadn't as yet been extinguished. The glow reminded me of why Egyptians had idolized the cat. The fascinating, warm light in its eyes suggested the sun and its life-giving ability. As it locked onto my gaze, it lifted its white whiskers in a tentative cat smile. Long eye teeth protruded like vampire fangs. This cat was both heart-breaking and mesmerizing.

There was no question that I had to make a decision ... right there and then. But I wasn't sure I wanted to. For fourteen years, since Sam, I had been on the go, never home, but now I was staying put. Was I ready for another cat? While I longed for that relationship, I didn't want to take the step.

Of course, I was kidding myself. I had no choice. There was absolutely no decision for me to make. I was an unreconstructed animal person. I already knew what I was going to do, despite my twinges of conflict over having another animal. For me there was no way I was not going to do all I could to rescue this poor creature, help it recover and enjoy whatever time it had left ... with me.

In the time since Sam I had also totally forgotten how cats operated. They gamed the system. This meant they would bend the human-created "rules" to get what they wanted. They did not accept the "human as universal standard" that humans did. But their behavior was nothing so uncouth as to be considered manipulation. No, it was just that cats adhered to a slightly different survival and life manual. My decision to adopt this cat was, in truth, *not* my decision at all. It was the cat's decision. Unlike dogs, cats rule. In their independence, they do what they want and "convince" you to go along with it, even if it is with the last strength they possess.

It flashed through my mind that being a relatively rational human being, I would soon have to accept, adapt, and accommodate to the fact that everyday decisions concerning this cat were likewise not mine to make. There was no ownership here on my part. I could choose to think of it as a partnership which was more like it. However, the cat was the senior partner. In actuality, this cat would *own* me. Moreover, this cat, or any cat for that matter, would hold the power of the veto at its command at any time, over almost any issue (except medical). This wasn't just a human perception. This was an unalterable fact of the Cat's Code and of life

So in those few seconds of watching the cat walk toward me my gut, emotion, logic—and the cat—told me this was to be my new companion. I was not going to be able to be that non-animal-person any longer. As a result, I allowed myself to feel very virtuous in making this momentous rescuing decision. That is, until as I reached into the car to get a blanket from the back seat, that I always kept for emergencies, in which to wrap this refugee.

It was then the cat glibly demonstrated whose decision it really was. Slipping past me, it shakily hopped in. Immediately curling up on the passenger seat, it fell asleep as if this were a regular occurrence. My jaw hung open as my thoughts tumbled hither, thither, and yon. The light came on in my head, albeit very slowly. I had my "aha!" Suddenly I was a kitty mom again. There was no question about it. It was etched in granite. A smile creased my cheeks in competition with the frown that creased my forehead. "Well, kiddo, I guess that settles that," I said aloud. Then I mumbled to myself, "Here we go again, ready or not."

CHAPTER 2

BEING OWNED BY A CAT

✷✷

I'm sure this truth must have been jackhammered some place in small letters on the stone tablets Moses brought down from Mount Sinai: Cats rule and humans should never forget it. "Okay," I whispered, "if you're comfy, we'll have to go get you some essentials." As the cat snored noisily, I shook my head, acknowledging I had a lot to re-learn about cats in general and learn about this cat in particular. I hoped it would come back fast. This little guy was clearly already several steps ahead of me.

After we left Goodnow, we turned right onto Rt. 20 and further up the road into the parking lot of the nearby supermarket. There I purchased a small bag of Purina cat chow, to see if he liked it—at least I remembered cats can be very finicky about their food—six cans of wet food, a water bowl and food dish, a deep, wide dishpan for litter, and a ten-pound bag of clay—cats can be equally finicky about their litter. I made a mental note: Get a cat carrier ... ASAP.

Two miles later I quietly glided into my garage and closed the garage door. Simultaneously I opened the passenger side door and the door to the house. The straggly stranger roused, unsteadily jumped out of the car, and trotted straight into the house. I shrugged my shoulders and laughed. I called after the cat, "I was going to say 'Welcome to your new home.' But I guess that's superfluous now." I saw its tail twitch.

As I always had done in the past, I talked aloud to the cat then took on both sides of the conversation. That was until the cat indicated to me that I had misinterpreted its intentions or desires.

First things first, I set up "his" cat pan in the bathroom off the kitchen and his filled food and water dishes on the light gray linoleum kitchen floor near the sink. Then I checked on my wandering unkempt guest to re-direct him to the kitchen. "Him?" Well, yes, I had checked its external apparatus because cats have indicated to me in the past that they don't like to be sexually mislabeled. He was continuing his wobbly tour of the premises, weaving in and out of rooms on both levels.

There was nothing shy about his demeanor which surprised me. He had obviously been on his own for a long time: avoiding dogs, owls, raccoons, cars, cat-hating people, and mean children, from toddlers to teens. I imagined his life had been very tricky, with injury, illness, or death always moments or inches away. He was obviously a survivor.

As he explored his new digs, I sat at my round cherry kitchen table, pen in hand. Trying to think of an appropriate name was a pain. I knew I couldn't call him, "Here, kitty." That would be seen as disrespectful. Cats were big on being respected since their days of having achieved their Egyptian god-like status.

The reason naming cats was no easy task is that their names have to reflect their personalities. They could not be just some word or label I liked. Our relationship would be starting out on the wrong foot if I stuck him with some unfitting moniker. Naming dogs, hamsters, bunnies, lizards, and birds was so much easier because they seemed to acknowledge and respond to whatever you threw at them. "Here, Herman, Bozo, Fluffy, Tarzan, Doofus, Xanadu, or Tricky Woo." Not so, in my experience, with cats.

Moreover, one of the things I had to keep in mind was how this name would sound in public ... if somehow the cat got out. Searching for it, calling its name aloud, would I embarrass myself and the cat by calling, "Here, Parkyakarkus, Mother's Darling Sweetheart, Ratso Rizzo, Lord Fautleroy, or Ferlinghetti?" I shivered at the thought.

My list would have been quite long if I hadn't quickly rejected all the inappropriate, commonplace, cute, and funny names. This cat was no "Cat-Astrophe" or "Mouser" or "FurBall or "Dracula" (because of his fangs). He had a dignity that needed to be expressed in his name. I started with historical figures like "Rasputin," "Raskolnikov," and "Churchill." Then I moved on to literary figures like "Sherlock," "Count Vronsky," and "Mr. Darcy." Next came authors like "Steinbeck," "Hemingway," and "Dostoevsky," and opera characters like "Giovanni," "Falstaff," and "Faust."

When he wandered back into the kitchen, he gravitated to the food and water. But surprisingly he was very insouciant about seeming hungry. He ate delicately but, unquestionably, did not pause. As he dined, I decided to run names past him. Mostly he ignored me. Instead, he concentrated on what might have been his first real meal in a very long time.

Approaching the end of my non-exhaustive list, I mentioned "Steinbeck," "Hemingway," "Dostoevsky", and "Faulkner." As they floated in the air, his head either drooped a fraction of an inch or gave no response. Was that a "no"? I was getting desperate. "How about Giovanni?" "Siegfried?" "Albrecht?" "Rudolfo?" I waited for a reaction. Nothing. "Falstaff?" His ears flattened almost imperceptibly.

Sighing, I gave up. This was getting boring and frustrating. "Come on. You're going to have to help me here. What should I call you? At this point I guess you wouldn't be interested in 'Faust' either." But at that name his ears twitched. I remembered how much cats communicated with their ears. "Really? 'Faust'?" He looked at me. "Are you really, really sure?" He seemed to lift his whiskers. But was he cleaning the cat food off his fangs or telling me "yes"?

"Well, I have to say you do look as if you must have made a deal with the devil to have kept you alive for this long. Okay, Faust, let's find you a place to sleep." He smiled with what seemed like sly amusement and followed me. It was as if he was "letting me" make him his bed which I created with towels on the floor of the bathroom off the kitchen. I reminded myself that I needed to get him a real kitty bed as well.

Too soon old and too late smart. It was once again obvious that I hadn't had a cat in a while. *I* was going to tell him where he would sleep? How dumb could I be? He was the one who would determine that. And he would do it on his own, thank you very much. He was a cat. He was the epitome of independent decision making, irrespective of his current condition. And, he made it quite apparent that while he might be allowing me to take him in, that did not mean he was any less in control of the decisions that affected his life. I would have to get that message soon and shape up if this were to work out between us.

As was all too predictable, after I went to bed, he joined me there. He snuggled up behind my knees as I slept on my side. Of course, this was to be only one of his many sleeping places. Consequently, it would soon be important for me to recognize that I had my side of the bed and he had ... both sides and top and bottom. This became never so obvious as when he went to bed first, leaving me to find a way to crawl in beside him or around him or sleep someplace else on the bed so as not to disturb him.

My pretzelizing myself for him made no sense to non-cat humans. In fact, they rolled their eyes back into their heads and looked to Heaven as if I were two cards short of a full deck. But others who were also held captive by a cat nodded their heads in embarrassing acknowledgment. This was something they shared only with those who were likewise blessed ... and cursed.

Sunday morning greeted us with a the slanting rays of the summer sun that made everything appear sharp, crystalline, and dipped in saturated color. The evening before had seemed like a dream, all miasmic and fragmented. I threw my legs over the side of the bed, stretched, and looked down. There lay lots of little rice grain-like particles on the navy-blue bedspread.

With my glasses in place on closer inspection I noted that some were making a writhing motion. Oh, no! I remembered that I had a cat ... and he obviously didn't live alone within his own skin. He had tapeworm. "Ooh, gross!" I scrunched up my face in disgust.

But that was not the worst of it. After I slipped on my moccasins lying on the floor beside the bed, I nearly stepped in a small pool of vomit. But not just any vomit. Oh, no. This was more than clear stomach juices on the wooden floor, at the edge of the two-by-three navy throw rug. In it lay eight elongated, thin, pale round, still-mobile worms.

This was even grosser. I shivered at the thought of having to manually pick them up to save them for Faust's first visit to the veterinarian. "Thank you, Faust," I called, "for being kind enough to share your intestinal parasites with me." But he was nowhere to be seen. Maybe he was too embarrassed to show his face after all that. I thought he should be. But more likely he was stationed in the kitchen patiently awaiting his breakfast.

Putting on vinyl gloves and gathering plastic sandwich bags to hold his fellow travelers, I scooped them up from the bedspread and floor then wiped the floor with a paper towel. Of all the truly revolting things I have had to handle in my life time, these round worms were right at the top of my list. Well, actually they shared first place with maggots that result from flies having deposited their eggs in not-totally-closed garbage bags of used cat litter. On the nausea rating scale cleaning cat pans or wiping up hairballs paled by comparison.

It was 6:30 a.m., morning shower time. When I went into the bathroom, I closed the door behind me. After touching the round worms, even with a glove which I quickly had thrown away, I felt I especially needed one. No sooner had I adjusted the water to the right temperature and soaked and lathered my hair, than I heard a heavy thumping at the bathroom door. It sounded like a police battering ram with a pillow lashed to its working end. My first paralyzing thought was that a SWAT team had crashed through the front door into the wrong house looking for a criminal. I was in imminent danger of being hauled away naked to the county jail. Shampoo suds running into my eyes, I rapidly switched off the shower to listen more carefully. There was no sound.

As I grabbed a towel to wipe my eyes and cover my body, I had the impression the door knob moved. "Don't shoot!" I shouted. "I'm unarmed." That's when a strange guttural noise started. Was that someone speaking? It reminded me of the voice at the other end of an obscene phone call. I waited another moment. This time I knew. It was Faust "mouhwing." Up to this point, I hadn't heard Faust make a sound, aside from his snoring. This was no ordinary meow. This was a gravelly, low-pitched, one-syllable breathy sound, something akin to what I'd imagined a baby bear with a cold would have sounded like. Since there was no trampling of feet, loudly-whispered instructions, or guns being cocked outside the door, I called, "Faust, is that you?"

I stepped gingerly out of the tub-shower, dripping on the glazed beige tiled floor, tightening the towel I was holding around me, and slapped my feet over to open the door. Faust rushed in as if he were going to save me from a fire or from the home invaders. He moved his head from side to side, looking for flames or smoke. Cautiously looking around the door, I saw we were alone. Maybe they had given up gone out for doughnuts.

Sighing, I was about to comfort him about his concerns for my safety when that glimmer in his amber eyes clued me in. It was not about me. It was about his not wanting me out of his sight. And, even more to the point, I hadn't given him his breakfast yet. He had been waiting, he wanted me to know, oh-so patiently for it, so when was I going to do something about it?

I looked him the eyes, "Do us both a favor. Don't do that again." I closed the door and asked, "Now that you're here, do you want to stay in here while I finish my shower?" He looked up at me with that "I knew you'd understand" expression. Then he seemed to do a double-take. He curled his upper lip and inched away from me, as the white foamy stuff on my head was now running down my shoulders and back. His reaction seemed to ask, You don't have rabies, do you?

Assuring him I'd be only a few more minutes, I stepped back into the shower, turned it on, and adjusted it to my previously comfortable temperature. He started his mouhwing again. Now what? I looked around the white vinyl shower curtain. He had his paws stretching upward against the door to clasp the handle to get out. "Are you going to be this way every time I take a shower?" I turned off the water again. "We were going to have to discuss this shower business."

What Faust the Dancing Cat Taught Me

Shaking my head, I acceded to his demands. I stepped out again and opened the door. He walked out calmly and I quickly hopped back into the shower before he started throwing himself against my closed door again. This, plus his parasites, made for an inauspicious start.

As I finished blow-drying my hair, he followed me into the bedroom where I dressed, or, attempted to dress. He sat on the bed watching as I pulled a beige cotton-blend blouse and a pair of tan linen slacks out of the closet. He cocked his head to one side and looked up at me as if to say, Are you sure you want to wear that? I held the pieces of attire out in front of me, inspecting them. They looked okay to me. Colors, styles, fabrics, and patterns were all right. Nothing clashed.

I frowned, wondering what he might have found wrong with the combination. Then I caught myself. Smacking my forehead with the heel of my hand, I asked aloud, "Why am I taking fashion advice from a cat? Especially from a cat who does not even know me yet?"

I shook my head again but still pulled out a light blue Oxford cloth shirt. To this he tapped his tail. Apparently that would do. Oh, thank you so much, Faust, I thought. As I began to dress in his sanctioned attire, Faust jumped down from the bed to wander into the kitchen to continue to await his breakfast.

I arrived shortly thereafter to find him standing by his canned food bowl. When I appeared, he walked over and tapped me on the foot then walked back to nudge his bowl toward me. "Okay, I read you loud and clear. You want breakfast." Looking at my small supply of cans, I asked, "How about some chicken and liver?" His dirty ears perked up, letting me know he approved that vintage without needing a sommelier to taste it first.

He received half a can with the remainder covered in aluminum foil and placed in the refrigerator for his dinner. I had a small bowl of granola with fresh peach slices, and cranberry juice on it. I didn't drink milk, eschewing most animal products which made eating a varied and tasty diet difficult to do.

I had read how much grain and water it took to produce one pound of beef and how many people you could feed with that amount of grain and water. Given the number of malnourished and starving people in this country and around the world, I decided I was not going to eat beef any longer. Maybe it wouldn't make any difference to the starving people, but it would make a difference to me—the principle of the thing. But then I'd see a large pizza covered in several cheeses, sausage, and pepperoni and drool. But it wasn't just the grain versus meat. I was increasingly becoming more aware of the horrifying abuses of factory animals as well as the antibiotics and steroids fed to them. This meant that eating any animals or their products was potentially dangerous health-wise as well as sacrilegious. Still I lusted body and soul for pizza.

As far as I was concerned, others could eat whatever they wanted—if they didn't mind being cannibals. While I was being sanctimonious, Faust could not be. He needed meat to get the important nutrients that were less available in dry, grain-dense food. However, if he could have been a vegetarian ...

Finding meat substitutes was difficult although grain products designed to do that were beginning to come onto the market. To get them and other organic products I had to drive twenty miles to Bread and Circus in Brookline. And they weren't half bad. But I would not go so far as to say they were "incredibly satisfying." Fortunately the quality and variety improved over the years. However, this was well before I discovered that I was wheat- and gluten intolerant, which accounted for my recurring urgent and painful gastrointestinal problems. That, of course, made dietary choices even more interesting. Although, if the truth be known, I would occasionally, under cover of darkness, break vegetarian rank and eat fish or seafood. It always left me feeling a little guilty but I justified it by convincing myself I was not getting enough protein otherwise. Naturally, at that time, many fishing locations, deep-sea and otherwise, began to have noticeable heavy metal and other types of pollution. I threw caution to the wind and took the risk.

As soon as Faust finished his breakfast, he jumped onto the cherry wood captain's chair across from me ... and waited for me to finish. "Look," I said, addressing him in a firm but respectful voice, "when I'm taking a shower, you can come into the bathroom. But if you do, you have to stay in until I finish. I have no intention of letting you in then letting you out again. And I certainly have no intention of repeating the process multiple times. Are we clear?"

He looked at me briefly, not even bothering to feign surprise, lifted his right paw, licked it, and began washing his face. "Are you listening to me?" He continued his ablutions. "Can we compromise on this?" No response. "How about this: If you want to be in the bathroom with me but don't like the sound of the shower, I can try taking a tub instead. Then you can come in and stay in until I'm finished. What do you say to that?"

He stopped his toilette and jumped down. I guessed that was that. But something in the back of my mind was nagging at me. It was coming back. Ah, yes. All our "compromises" were, thus far, being made by me. I was acting like a typical human cat-companion. I was already bending over backwards for someone who had been in my house about twelve hours and who had given me so far, in exchange, only his alimentary parasites. I had to ask myself: Was I going to allow him to dictate to me? I most assuredly wouldn't respond to another human like that. But this was different. It didn't take much contemplation to see the answer was a likely ... "yes."

CHAPTER 3

WORKING TOGETHER
✳✳

The rest of the day was quiet with Faust rolling on my papers on my desk in my office. I was editing a to-be-self-published mystery novel for grammar, syntax, spelling, continuity, voice, and pace. This was about a female psychologist in San Francisco who is sitting in a movie theater, watching a thriller. Next to her a stranger falls over dead from an injection of succinylcholine in his neck.

Of course, it takes everyone some time to discover what killed the man because it's the perfect murder tool. This poison which relaxes all the muscles, including those necessary for breathing, requires only a small effective dose. It has ease of administration and rapid action. Moreover, it is exceedingly difficult to detect by a forensic team because it metabolizes quickly. It's certainly quicker than an assassination by a ricin-filled pellet which was shot into the Bulgarian dissident and writer Georgi Markov, in 1978, by an umbrella-gun.

Next I worked around Faust on composing an outline for a training manual for first-line managers. These are supervisors who are one-step removed from the work force they direct. Often these people were seen as particularly talented workers who had then been promoted to do something they may or may not be as talented to do. It never seems to occur to companies that workers and managers have and use different skill sets.

What makes a worker good at his or her job does not necessarily make that person as a supervisor good at his or her job. Besides, having been one of the "gang" and then stepping into a managerial position is hard for both the other workers and the new supervisor. Resentments can occur. This could be a complex program to write if managers and promoted workers truly understood the obstacles that promoted workers had to meet successfully.

However, that was not the thrust of this educational piece. This was to deal more simply with what a worker-becoming-a-supervisor should do when becoming a first-line manager. Issues having to do with the psychological and social transition from worker to manager were not to be discussed as if they don't exist or were not important. The program was not geared to help anyone who discovered that this promotion was not what anyone had anticipated or desired.

While a company wants someone who knows the business to be a supervisor, it needs to determine that the person has the supervisory and leaderships skills, the knowledge of what is entailed in the job, as well as the desire to lead. Having an experienced supervisor come in from the outside who then can learn the product-related business is another approach that can reduce the potential problems with psychological and social transitions. However, for this course, who cared? That was totally beside the point.

For an autobiography I had received, I had to create a rough estimate of how long it would take to edit it and make literary suggestions about it. When the phone rang, I was too engrossed to hear it. Faust patted me on the cheek with his paw as if to say, Pay attention. Turn off that offensive noise.

It was a question from the pharmaceutical firm about my suggestions for a mailing piece to physicians. I had sent them an illustration which suggested using a half-tone photograph of a female's face with a target super-imposed over the eye. The objective was to focus on and talk about targeting and protecting the dry eye during surgery with their eye lubricant.

Considering Faust's state of health and his life of roughing it, he struck me as particularly friendly, gentle, and playful. However, I would have preferred he played using his back feet to attack something other than the novel's type-written manuscript which was lying by my typewriter. When I returned it to the author, I didn't want to have to explain the Braille-like holes along the margins, scratch marks and tears between paragraphs, and occasional pieces of 3M invisible tape. A freelance writer/editor does have professional standards to maintain. That doesn't include explaining cat playful behavior with their personal writing.

To distract him I went to the bedroom, found a knee-length sock, tied a knot in the center of it, went back to my office, and gave it to him. Mindlessly, I didn't think to put in on the floor first. That goof undoubtedly gave him permission to stay on my desk, on the manuscript, to wrestle with the sock, preventing me from turning the pages. By the time I put him and the sock on the floor, he was no longer interested in it. Instead, he hobbled into the kitchen to wait for lunch. I was getting smarter but way too slowly.

We had lunch on the screened-in back porch which overlooked the heavily-treed backyard, abundant with grass, squirrels, and birds. For the moment, he ignored me. Crouching on the floor, ears back, he chattered at the squirrels that came near the screen. They happily mocked his lack of access to them. They dared him to chase them. When the futility of his position dawned on him, he decided to resume his dignity by taking on the role of royal food taster. I had no doubt this was deemed to protect me from being poisoned by my enemies at court. These would-be enemies who obviously hadn't as yet learned about succinylcholine.

He pawed and sniffed everything on my plate. "Oh, no you don't!" I immediately grabbed him. "Sorry, Faust, this will not do: I will not have you on the table touching my food." I sternly put him down. This was an unthinking move on my part.

Apparently, my putting him down likewise would not do as far as he was concerned. He clawed his way back up my pant leg, seemingly taking his time ascending. His claws stuck in my flesh like pitons in rock. He was making sure I received the message loud and clear. In his book my putting him down was not acceptable human-cat behavior.

We would have to talk about this too. At this rate, I was going to have to keep a notebook and pen with me at all times to keep track of the exponential number of topics we would have to discuss to straighten him out on what was "acceptable" behavior in *my* house. *My* house? That was increasingly becoming a laugh.

That day was uneventful except for the fact I had made the mistake of leaving out a wooden step ladder when I went to answer the phone. I had used it to put some infrequently-used pots and pans away in the maple kitchen cabinet above the refrigerator. Faust may have been skeletal and wobbly, but he could, and did, make his way up the ladder to the top. When I returned to the ladder, he was surveying his domain. He rotated his head ninety degrees to the right, then on hundred eighty degrees in the left, reminding me of a beacon in a lighthouse. Taking in everything from this fresh vantage point, he seemed to be enjoying this heady experience. I, on the other hand, was feeling my palms sweat. For heaven's sake, don't fall!

Concerned about his balance problem and possibly falling from such a height, I tried coaxing him to come down. "Faust, how would you like a nice brushing?" I held an old hairbrush in my hand and waved it at him. He was too busy looking around. "If you come down now, I'll give you a good scratching too." He looked at me momentarily as if to say dismissively, Not right now, maybe later. He indicated he would come down when he was ready. But ... I should hold that offer open until that time.

Now what should I do? Climb up the ladder and unceremoniously snatch him from his perch? Or let him come down by himself? His going up could be lots easier than his coming down. I wasn't so sanguine about his ability to descend it. I made a mental note to myself: get a cat tree, a tall one with lots of little hidey-holes and platforms. He was going to need places to climb and places to hide when he recovered. So I decided to compromise. I stayed in the kitchen so every few minutes I could check on him out of the corner of my eye, like a mother hen trying to corral and tuck her scurrying newborn chicks under her breast feathers. I knew he was catching me checking on him, undoubtedly feeling satisfied he had things (that is *me*) under control.

Later when I glanced toward the ladder, at least for the tenth time, I could see him change position, look around, and decide to descend. I started to move toward the ladder, to be ready to catch him should he fall. I expected him to jump onto the counter then onto the floor. But this process I felt was fraught with dangers because of his frailty. Instead, he amazed me. He carefully walked down the ladder face-first. That was totally unexpected. I had idea he had the strength or ingenuity to do that.

As I was continually to discover, he often did the unexpected. Every time he did something new, I had to re-assess my assumptions about what he would or could do. Being human and a supposedly "superior creation," I was not altogether thrilled with being wrong and humbled so often. It meant that if I were smart, I would not judge any cat—but this cat in particular—by my human standards.

That evening, having finished my writing and an early dinner, I snuggled into the sofa to watch Masterpiece Theater on PBS. They were showing the first run of the thirteen episodes of "I, Claudius" with Derek Jacobi as the stuttering, disabled child who would later become a Roman senator. I called Faust, "You don't want to miss this. Did you know that the Romans did not hold cats up as deities the way the Egyptians did? I suspect you won't see a single cat in this series."

He sauntered in from somewhere, hoisted himself onto the cushions beside me, and looked askance at me as if to say, So what? I continued my monologue, "If Livia had had a cat, you could have been a perfect match for her."

Before I could explain what I meant by my unintentionally sarcastic-sounding comment, he gave a cursory glance at the TV screen and seemingly questioned what precisely I had meant by that. Then he immediately rejected my assessment of any conceivable resemblance between the treacherously manipulative wife of

Augustus Caesar and himself. Miffed that one who should be worshipped could be so compared, he moved to the other end of the sofa. There he fell into his noisy sleep without so much as a by your leave.

I realized too late I'd have to be careful about what I said to him. He might not understand the exact words, but he was apparently very sensitive to how I said things. He could detect attitude by the nuanced sounds and any accompanying gestures. Before going to bed, I left a message on the veterinarian's answering machine that I had someone that needed to see him and I'd call for an appointment in the morning. I had known him from when he cared for Sam.

Before I called Dr. Jeffrey Katuna at the Wellesley-Natick Veterinary Hospital on Monday to set up Faust's appointment, I tried an experiment. At 6:30 a.m. I filled the tub to see what would happen as a result of "our" agreement about my not taking showers. I called Faust and waited for him to wander in before I closed the door. At least, I hoped, that was better than my having to get out of the tub to open the door for him. I stripped off my extra-tall man's red tee-shirt I used as my nightgown and stepped into the water. It brought back memories of past loungings in the tub, letting stress ebb away with the movement of the warm, soothing water.

CHAPTER 4

VISITING THE VET

✷✷

It had been years since I had taken a tub. Generally, I preferred a quick shower. Once soaking in the water, I tended to stay there far too long. I'd begin to think about things I needed to do and things I wanted to do. My mind would wander to someday tearing myself from work and actually taking a vacation. I envisioned a road trip across the country, visiting the national parks, from the Rockies to Yosemite, one by one. It sounded so appealing. So when I finally came out of the water, I always looked pale and exceedingly shriveled, like a floater having been pulled from the Boston Harbor by a police grappling hook. Yeech. But at least I wasn't bloated ... and I was clean.

I had no sooner settled myself into the luxuriously, body-caressing water than Faust jumped onto the narrow rim of the old-fashioned white porcelain cast-iron tub, replete with ball and claw feet. Because the tub was placed against the wall, only two-thirds of its perimeter was available to him on which to balance. But that seemed more than sufficient.

As I eyed him warily, he began to leisurely walk its boundary, turning shakily around at each wall to retrace his steps. He stopped once. Leaning precariously over the water, he began to knead my shoulders which were against the tub end opposite the faucet. Did he slip, land on my shoulders, and knead them because he was there? Or did he choose to lean over to do it? That was an unexpected but delightful surprise. A little longer would have been nice. Though totally retracted claws would have been even nicer.

Suddenly he started to sing. I'm not sure what else you could call it. I won't insult him by calling it a caterwaul, because it had none of that raucous sexual undertone—but it was close to it. Cats make all kinds of sounds. They have a wide range of vocalizations from mews, meows, chirps, growls, hisses, murmurs, and shrieks to chatters, caterwauls, and moans. Singing is different but I'm not sure how you would characterize it. To be charitable I thought it sounded vaguely like a feline Louis Armstrong singing Rodolfo's aria "Che gelida manina" from Puccini's First Act of *La Bohème*. It resonated throughout the small bathroom, bouncing off the walls. With only a bathmat and a couple of towels to dampen the vocalization, Faust's singing resounded.

He was crooning to me, or so I fantasized. He reminded me of a strolling troubadour as his body moved to the music with romantic feeling. I wondered if he were showing his appreciation for my deep-sixing the shower. Or maybe he was repaying me for my St. Francis of Assisi-like rescue of him. After five minutes my ears began to ring. I told him, "That was lovely, Faust, and thanks for the massage. You are such a good boy. But I have to rinse my hair in the shower now," as I pointed to it. "You may want to get down." He looked up, lifted his whiskers, and jumped down. I rinsed as quickly as I could before he could start Gene Krupa-drumming "Big Noise From Winnetka" on the door to get out.

Doing a lot of research of cat books later at the library, I found absolutely nothing about cat singing. I had heard someone say some place at some time that this tub singing behavior wasn't something all that unusual among cats, but I had never had one do it before. This person apparently thought there were, may have been a few cats around the globe that tightrope-walked around tubs, belting out a ballad or two for their human companions. But this person was given to elaborating on the truth on occasion. And that did make for a good story.

Truth or myth, I couldn't document it with only one example. Even if his performance were not totally unique to him as a cat, it didn't really matter. What Faust did was for *me* ... and for me alone. It felt very special ... despite the decibels.

From then on I took baths. Every bath thereafter he treated me to his strolling Italian serenade, *sans* guitar. Each time he made small variations which kept it sounding fresh. Although, sometimes it sounded more like "Shake Your Booty" by KC and the Sunshine Band played at sixteen and two-thirds rpm.

When I called Dr. Katuna, described Faust's obvious conditions, he indicated I could bring him in that morning. Luck was truly with us. Our appointment was for eleven o'clock. Faust, however, didn't share my enthusiasm. Since I still needed a real cat carrier, I had to improvise. I used a medium-sized box. On the sides of it I created silver-dollar-sized air holes with a serrated knife. When done, I inelegantly scooped him up and shoved him into it. With a final flourish, I crisscrossed two pieces of duct tape across the folded top to slow down his escape.

Of course, I was being exceedingly optimistic ... and I knew it. Any motivated adult cat worth its weight in salt can shred a cardboard box in no time at all. Retrieving my plain brown paper bag containing the sealed plastic sandwich bags of tapeworm segments and roundworms from the refrigerator, I shuttled Faust off to his appointment.

From the moment I had grabbed him, he mouhwed his wheezy protestations long and loud. I was amazed at the volume he could achieve given his seeming upper respiratory problem. He acted as if his rescuer, who I thought should receive several gold stars for caring and helping, were about to stretch him on a torturer's rack. Insulted, I thought his behavior seemed all out of proportion to the situation. Where was the gratitude I deserved and was due? Claws rapidly scraped the inside of the top of the box. I could hear his disgruntled mumbling about not belonging in there. This was no way to show my respect for his ancestry.

The gist was he was reminding me of his descending from royalty, in case I didn't know my history. *We royals*, despite how he looked at the moment, were not, under any circumstances, to be treated like the common herd. He most assuredly deserved better than this and would remind me of the same whenever it was necessary!

Fortunately we didn't have to wait long to see Dr. Katuna because his clinic waiting room was full of curious dogs, not as restrained as they should have been on their leashes. More than one attempted to rub its wet nose on Faust's box as it sniffed it and then tried to wriggle its face inside it. I had to push them away. Looking through one of the air holes, I could see how put-upon Faust felt. It was clear he was debating whether to make himself invisible in a corner ... or to self-righteously tear off their nostrils as they intruded into his space. Fortunately he chose not to perform a canine nasalectomy.

Once on the examining table, however, he resumed his calm, confident, superior demeanor. In fact, he seemed to enjoy the vet looking him over ... except, of course, for taking his temperature. That was undignified but something he would choose to endure. He didn't yet know if he could trust this tall male human. He held his bony head high as his species was expected to do and tolerated it with noblesse oblige.

Checking his ears, mouth, tail, abdomen, heart and lungs, and my plastic bags of parasitic worms, Dr. Katuna proclaimed Faust had ear mites, tapeworm, roundworm, and fibrous-sounding lungs. Next he did an x-ray, which required considerable restraint on Faust's part. Lying on a cold glass plate, not moving, while a large, imposing whirring machine slithered over him, tested his patience. But it did reveal that at one time he had had a bad pulmonary infection which had left his lungs able to work at only half-efficiency. So

What Faust the Dancing Cat Taught Me

how he pulled a Placido Domingo imitation on the bathtub rim I'll never know.

His heart and kidneys were in reasonably good, but not great, shape. His overall condition bespoke dehydration and malnutrition. There was no doubt he was in starvation mode. His body was essentially breaking down his own tissue in order to try to survive. This was not helped by the competitive intestinal worms that gorged themselves on any nourishment he could ingest. Dr. Katuna gave him two hundred milliliters of sub-cutaneous fluids and his first de-worming pill before he left.

Over the next ten days Faust and I repeatedly did a heavily rhythmic dance from Stravinsky's "The Rite of Spring" ballet as I wrestled with him to try to slaughter his ear mites. This required me to hold his skull in place while I opened his ear canal. Then I used multiple cotton swabs to gently wipe out the heavy wads of blood and wax. To add insult to injury, I then had to insert Tresaderm droplets several times a day, without letting the droplets fall onto the floor, his fur, or in his eyes. Those miniscule mites are tough little insects to kill.

While I'm sure, in his more contemplative moments, he appreciated what I did, he chose not to make a big deal of showing it. At least, he was no longer shaking his head and vigorously scratching his ears. I preferred not to put on the plastic Elizabethan collar if I could avoid it. With it on eating was difficult. Drinking was difficult. Using the litter box was difficult. All he would have to do is lower his head at the wrong time and scoop up wet litter which would tumble toward his mouth, or worse.

After each "mauling," we each needed to go to our respective corners, not unlike in a boxing match. But our gladiatorial struggles actually had more of the dramatic razzle-dazzle of a professional wrestling match. Imagine Gorilla Monsoon versus Executioner #2. I'm sure it would have been something like the 1976 highly-promoted, World Wide Wrestling Federation's super-show, "Showdown at Shea Stadium" at Flushing, New York, but without the attendance of a crowd of 32,000.

CHAPTER 5

PILLING FOR FUN AND PROFIT
✳✳

Pilling for tapeworm and round worm continued for a short time at home. To be more precise it continued for way longer than it should have. Pilling is the stuff of mythology ... and legends. Even if you have never pilled a cat, you likely have heard tell of the bloody wars fought between *Homo sapiens* and *Felis catus* on the ancient Battlefield of Pilling. "Trying" is the operant word when it comes to slipping a pill down a cat's throat. Lawd, have mercy.

No matter what veterinarians and books by so-called experts tell you, it isn't as simple as wrapping the cat in a towel with only its head exposed, coaxing it to open its jaws, and gently popping the ball of medication down its throat. Maybe it works for those who are strangers to the cat. Maybe it works for those who can petrify the cat with a mere murderous glance. But it doesn't work for the person who waits on the cat, meeting its every whim, in its own home. There are masters and there are servants ... and never the twain shall meet.

The problem? First the towel is a dead giveaway that something nasty is afoot. Faust hightailed it for parts unknown when he saw me attempt to look totally uninterested in him as I held an open bath towel outside the bathroom. There was no way in heaven or hell that he was letting me near him. He knew the towel meant being trapped, held against his will, and having to submit to a human's control. Whether this was an innate response or, as I suspected, more likely to be something he had learned, I didn't know. And it didn't matter one iota.

Second was the fact that he had great social radar, a feline form of emotional intelligence. It made him mindful of what human intentions might be by carefully observing their body language. Even before he had spotted the towel, he was wary. And once the towel appeared, there was no point in going after him. This left me little choice about my next actions. As much as I didn't like the negative implications of sneaking up on him, I would likely have to try to craftily do the deed when he least expected it.

When I did catch him unawares, it wasn't long before I discovered that trying to manipulate the towel around the cat created more problems than it was worth. It was becoming obvious I would have to chuck this protective covering and risk having my arms clawed and shredded.

Leaving me bloodied but unbowed ... and, hopefully, successful. I didn't want to precipitate his fear and anger by suddenly grabbing him. Instead, I chose moments when he was relaxing.

I picked him up, placed him lovingly on my lap. Wedging his back into my left armpit, I held down his front paws with my left hand and tried to pry open his mouth with my right hand. Oops. My right hand also held the de-worming pill. Not being skilled at conjuring, I found I couldn't transfer the pill from my palm into his oral cavity without letting go of his jaw. The pill fell onto the carpet and rolled under the sofa. This was *déjà vu*. Sam came to mind and the loud, wrestle-chase-wrestle matches we had had years ago over the same operation.

The next time I tried I crept up on him, placed him on the floor in a sitting position facing in the direction I was. I kneeled over him. I let my left hand remain free to pry open his jaw so my right could pop in the pill. The only problem was his jaw would not cooperate. He would clench it closed and my left hand reaching around to his face had no leverage. Besides, I was deathly afraid of hurting him by using too much force. I didn't want to make this *mano y mano*.

I've found humans have a tendency to make this a battle between "equals" and get quite angry when the animals won't cooperate. They want to force them to do their will using all their strength. It hardly seemed fair to use my hundred and five pounds of strength against his only five pounds. Surely, I kidded myself, I could *out-think* this cat!

It reminded me all too well when my father's jaw had been broken by an overly-enthusiastic, albeit somewhat Neanderthal, dentist who was trying, unsuccessfully, to extract a molar. You'd think that the dentist having to plant his feet on the arms of the dental chair in order to gain purchase on the tooth might have had a clue that some other technique was truly necessary. I prided myself on being one-up when it came to dealing with cats. I knew working with them required significant patience, persistence, practice, and psychology ... mostly "cat" psychology ... and looking at the world from the cat's perspective. Well, as best I could being a mere human. But I did find a way to open his mouth without a bone chisel.

Of course, getting the jaw open was only half-way to success. Then there was the proper placement of the pill so it would actually go down. Cats are champion spit-ballers. They would be hailed for their prowess in any elementary school in America. The problem is that as the piller, you can think you have the pill at the back of the pillee's mouth. You are confidently massaging their throat to help them swallow it. But the moment you stop, out it flies. If you are lucky, it doesn't hit you in the eye or your mouth, get stuck in your favorite cashmere sweater, or land on the television screen.

Then there are other times that the pill hasn't been spit out. Swelling with pride, you congratulate yourself on a job well done. But as you look around, the cat is letting the now-soggy, slimy ball drop quietly to the floor as it walks away very satisfied with itself.

After too many frustrating sessions and lost or destroyed pills, I told Faust we had to come to some agreement. When I thought I had his attention, I said, "These worms have to go. They are gobbling up all your nourishment." I left out how disgusting I found them, especially if they were puked onto the sofa or bed or I stepped on them in my bare feet. "What do I have to do to get you to take the medication to get rid of them?" He cocked his head to the side, looked at me, then looked directly into the kitchen.

"What? You want me to bribe you?" He lifted his whiskers. "Look," I said, falling into the warm pools of his mischievous amber eyes, "I do not like bribery ... however, for this I'll give you a treat every time you take a de-worming pill. Will that work?" If cats can shrug, he shrugged. I took that as agreement.

He followed me into the kitchen. I retrieved a bag of cat treats from the upper cabinet and looked at him for confirmation of our deal. The pill went down quickly—at least I couldn't find it on the floor or stuck to his fur afterwards—followed by the treat and a kiss on the top of his head. "Good Faust." Problem solved ... this time.

However, if you have a small pill to give your cat that does not smell and/or taste positively obnoxious, you may be able to hide the pill in a small ball of soft food. This you feed to the cat by the finger-full. If you put the pill in the food and place it the cat's dish, the cat may be able to intentionally or unintentionally disengage the pill from its hiding place. Also, giving the food by hand is so much more intimate and sharing. Faust liked that as he could lasciviously lick my fingers afterwards.

Demolishing his intestinal parasites would finally let his cadaverous body fill out. Over several more carefully spaced-out vet appointments, for which he now had a carrier, he received his vaccinations and had his fur de-matted and washed. Unbeknownst to Faust, he also had an upcoming appointment for his reproductive organs to be rendered "neutral."

I didn't know how to explain to him that he was no longer going to be capable of siring kittens, but maybe at his advanced age that wasn't such a big deal. To my considerable surprise Dr. Katuna informed me that this ancient-looking feline was, in fact, only about one-year old. Now I was sure not to tell him about his upcoming snip-snip de-Tom-ing because of the inevitable ensuing argument.

By the day his surgery arrived, he was less wobbly, well on his way to gaining flesh on his bones, and looking more like the adolescent cat he was. Being a little healthier now, he was better able to tolerate the anesthesia. The evening before his surgery he knew there was something disquieting about to happen when his food dishes disappeared at six o'clock.

He mouhwed piteously as if he were being physically abused. Anyone outside the house hearing his torment would have called the authorities to haul me off to the pokey for animal cruelty. He would have sat on the back of his over-stuffed chair by the front window, looking vindicated as the cruiser pulled away.

If I wouldn't allow him to eat, he decided he would not allow me to sleep. Fair is fair. He eschewed cuddling with me. Instead, he spent the night sitting at the foot of the bed mouhwing and slapping my feet with his paws, as if he had a mouse under the covers he was playing with. Every time I dozed off, he mouhwed and slapped me some more, occasionally drawing blood on my toes.

Having to have him at the clinic by 7:45 a.m., I dragged myself bleary-eyed out of bed at six o'clock, showered in spite of him, and dressed as to my own liking. I grabbed a granola bar and located his carrier. I was very careful not to reveal the carrier to him. Instead I took him to it.

The look on his face when I grabbed him was a chilling indictment of typically-insensitive human intentions. He looked back at me with incomprehensible disdain as if to say, I know what you want to do. I've heard stories. No snip-snip for me. I have rights. I'm a male and I haven't passed on my genes yet. You need my permission and I am not about to grant it! Despite all my soothing reassurances that it would be over quickly with little discomfort, he was not assuaged. I wondered if he had an accounting book in which he registered all such cruel acts against him allegedly perpetrated by me.

That afternoon when I went to pick him up between four and six o'clock, he still lay like a limp ragdoll. I suspected his impaired lungs were taking longer to release the gas anesthesia. With his IV portal still intact on the shaved patch of his left front leg, he looked at me groggily. Only temporarily defeated, he seemed to say, You did it anyway, against my wishes, didn't you. How could you, you traitor? I expected better from you even if you are a human.

I felt guilty that he had to have the surgery. But it was necessary. I wasn't going to let him help contribute to cat over-population if he got out of the house. I stroked his head and commiserated, "I'm truly sorry I had to do that. I know you feel bad now but I promise you'll feel better soon. I'll help you feel better. I'll bet you're hungry." He raised his half-closed eyes toward me. They spoke with more than a little sarcasm, Why would I be hungry since you stole my food last night. You didn't leave me with even a nibble for nearly twenty-four hours. Then his head dropped and he drifted off again.

In his current stupor he was unlikely to be able to appreciate my sympathetic murmurings. I knew I would have to shower affection upon him to show him I really did care. I really was sorry for the temporary discomfort of his vacated nether region. Maybe he could ... and would ... forgive me in time.

At home, several hours later when he had finally recovered from his anesthesia, he condescended to casually sample some food. This was despite the fact he was starving. It was a matter of adhering to the strict dictates of the Cat's Code. The Code required that he always maintain control, or, at least, always give the impression of doing it. This was even when he didn't give a Rottweiller's butt about it because he so wanted to chow down, dammit. Being a cat was not always easy although he was loath to broadcast it. After another hour, he decided it would not hurt his image significantly to crawl into my lap to be petted and scratched and fawned over. He most assuredly deserved that attention after all he had been through.

CHAPTER 6

LEAVING HIM ALONE
✱✱

Once he no longer was shedding tapeworm segments or round worms, I allowed him to ride in the car occasionally, unencumbered by the cat carrier because of his pitiful crying. This was a calculated sound, guaranteed to break your heart or scrape dead cells from your sinuses. I did keep the carrier with us in the back seat at all times ... as a precaution. In a short time I discovered that going out only "occasionally" when I went out, was not what he had in mind.

He made it obvious that he didn't want to be left home alone ... period. Perhaps he had been abandoned, dumped, run away from abuse, or somehow managed to get lost. Now that he had a human to save and wait on him, he did not seem to want to be out of that person's sight. As I found out, that could be a real problem.

He tried to tell me this by twitching his tail and cocking his head to one side as I headed for the door. He raised his paws on the door jamb and looked back at me mournfully. But, much to his distress, I hadn't yet learned to accurately interpret what was underlying these actions. Humans can be so slow. And, despite his soon-to-be-blatant severe separation anxiety, he was not about to beg me not to leave him alone, as much as he may have wanted to.

However, he quickly found a more effective way to get my attention. He stopped eating whenever I left him alone. Only when I returned would he commence eating. That was both a visual and visceral announcement that if he were to get all the nutrition he needed to look like a real cat again, I would have to stop interfering with his recovery by leaving him all alone to pine.

This was not his acknowledgment that his fear of abandonment was taking over. Oh, no. Instead, he cleverly turned it around. It was *I* who was "forcing" him to be practical, to save his food just in case I didn't return. Being less smart than a cat, I didn't catch it until the second time around. When it happened again, I could see the anxiety in his body language. His eyes were open wide, pupils dilated, head down but scanning for information, with his ears flattened back. Now he also cowered with the tip of his tail moving slowly from side to side. Poor little thing, I cried out to myself.

I have to give him credit. He was exceedingly patient with me as I gradually learned what his body language was attempting to communicate in different situations. This was whether I deserved his patience or not. I'm sure his species had always had to be patient with other inferior species, like dogs. As a result of my own "cat-related developmental disability," I seemed to be doing a lot of apologizing and trying to get back on his good side.

Because of his anxiety, in his first month with me I incautiously risked taking him to the grocery store. Where O where was my head? Of course, doing so was going to be a big problem if I were caught. No animals, aside from service dogs, were allowed in food establishments. He obviously was not a seeing-eye dog, and unlikely to pass muster as a hearing-ear cat. Faust and I had come to an accommodation about his carrier. He would agree to enter it for short periods of time *if* I made it worthwhile for him afterward.

Conflicted, I finally said, Public health regulations be damned. I couldn't leave him alone like this. In the Stop 'n' Shop parking lot I put him in his carrier and placed it on the bottom shelf of a cart at the Cart Return. Before I had closed the lid, I had made him promise on his Cat's Honor (cross his furry heart and hope to die) to be quiet so no one would know he was there.

But, as usual, instead of agreeing, he focused on his paw and how to remove dust motes from between his splayed toes with his tongue. With some trepidation I rolled him into the store. He was quiet and no one was paying any attention to us. All was going well so far.

As we made our way down the raw produce aisle, I rolled over a spilled peanut in its shell which loudly cracked open and made the cart bump. But he was good to his word. He did not make a peep. I was still a little anxious about his starting to mouhw so I hurriedly picked up salad greens, the genetically-toughened, cardboard-tasting tomatoes, carrots, red and green bell peppers, and extra-firm tofu. Down the salad dressing aisle, I spotted Ken's Steakhouse and picked up Italian and oil and vinegar dressings.

At the end of the next aisle over a woman was giving out tiny samples of bratwurst on a toothpick. The aroma was strong. If I had still been a carnivore, my mouth would've watered so I worried how Faust was going to react. Increasing little tapping sounds manifested themselves and grew louder as scratching on the carrier sides commenced. The woman looked at me oddly, not sure if I had made the sounds and then wondering how and why I would have. I had to hustle.

"Would you like to taste a..."

I cut her off, smiling, "No thanks. Already eaten." I pushed the cart ahead of me. The scratching was getting even louder. "Faust," I whispered out of the right side of my mouth as I leaned casually over the cart, quickly checking to see if anyone were watching, "you have to be quiet."

At the end of two aisles over was another food tempter, offering cubes of real cheddar cheese, from the contented, grass-eating cows of California. Faust caught a whiff and started rapidly pawing the top of the carrier with increased enthusiasm. Oh, no. My stomach fluttered and tightened. I knew he was going to start mouhwing at any moment, drowning out the Muzak with the sounds of the baby bear in nasal distress. And of course, I was at the back of the store, still having to pass by the fresh fish counter.

"That's it, kiddo," I whispered again, but more harshly. "You're not coming to the grocery store again," which was something I had already decided because I couldn't stand the stress. With the aisle by the cheese man jammed, I practically ran past the fish counter to turn up the next aisle toward the front of the store and the registers.

Faust, inhaling deeply and undoubtedly picturing raw salmon, tilapia, cod, crab legs, and shrimp, was now jumping around in his carrier. I could see it rocking back and forth through the metal mesh of the cart. "You should never have come to the supermarket," I almost shouted. "You are never coming here again. There is going to be big trouble because of you." The pitch of my voice was rising. "Do you hear me!" I tried to look straight ahead and not at the carrier.

A woman with her young child seated in the front of her cart, a pacifier stuck in its mouth, was approaching me. I had not glanced up in her direction until that moment. She looked at me angrily as if she thought that I had been speaking accusingly to her. She frowned, squinted her eyes, and puckered her mouth. I could see she was getting ready to address my perceived abuse of her. But then she stopped. As I continued to mumble to myself, I wasn't really looking at her. My gaze was off in the distance—scanning the registers up front for a free one.

With raised eyebrows, she scrutinized me. Apparently she was trying to decide if maybe I was one of those who wasn't cooking on all four burners. She had undoubtedly heard about people who shouted and talked to themselves. So maybe this was not the time for her to respond. Maybe verbally assaulting me wasn't such a good move after all. Instead, she looked down and hurriedly passed me to continue on her way. There was safety in numbers at the busy poultry counter fifteen feet behind me.

By the time I reached the only open register with no one ahead of me, Faust had calmed down. My heart was pulsing out of my chest, my temples were throbbing, and my shoulder muscles were going into spasm. I was on the verge of a migraine. Fortunately the cashier was busy with paperwork, charting cash register receipts. Preoccupied, she did not seem to recognize my crimson cheeks and neck or notice Faust's carrier.

I quickly unloaded my few items onto the conveyor belt, paid cash, and walked with purpose out of the store. Once in the car, I opened the carrier to chastise Faust for his most unseemly behavior. But before I could open my mouth to explain the facts of life about keeping his word of silence, he leapt out onto my lap. Kneading my legs a couple of times, he reached up, licked my face, and bunted his head against my chest.

"Smart aleck," I said, "now what am I going to do after that?" I swear he smiled at that. Needless to say, I snuggled with him but I didn't try taking him to Stop 'n' Shop, or any other food market, again. The stress was sure to precipitate a coronary or stroke.

What it all came down to was that he was going to be my traveling companion *nearly* every time I went out. I emphasized "nearly" because it obviously would depend upon my destination. Practically speaking, there were going to be times when he would have to stay on his own at home. Slowly becoming a better student of cat psychology, I created ways to make him feel less anxious about our infrequent separations. At those times, I focused on him. I made a big deal out of semi-strenuous play time with him before I left, like getting him to chase the Wiffle ball around the rooms.

Then I repeated the ritual as soon as I returned home. I left the television on for him, especially if I could find animals programs or movies he liked. I gave him catnip. I played classical music after determining what he particularly liked. He had a penchant for harp and Mozart. I even recorded a tape of my speaking to him in an affectionate way—you know all the embarrassing soft cooing that human cat parents make—with breaks between the messages, and played it on my tape recorder as a continuous loop. That helped ... at least a little.

CHAPTER 7

GOING OUT
✳✳

As we traveled more, he rapidly came to the conclusion that the passenger seat was no longer going to work for him. It was comfortable enough but it wasn't close enough to me or high enough to see out. Therefore, it was time for him to assume his rightful place on my lap. There he could knead my thighs with his front paws then stand on his hind legs to look out the windshield through the steering wheel or out the driver's side window.

From here he would respond with royal decorum, *sans* the imperial wave—I'd have to add that—whenever someone in another car or on the sidewalk noticed and pointed—which was often. He made himself available to his public and flourished in the attention.

After only a few weeks of my retracing our route back home from trips to the vet, I found Faust getting excited when we were about a half-mile from the house. He started prancing in my lap, doing a feline version of a schottische, looking eagerly around, taking in every house and side road we passed.

As we actually approached the house, he ran back and forth from my lap to the passenger seat. He hopped onto the dashboard and peered intently through the windshield. When the car finally stopped, he lifted his whiskers, as he had at the library when he introduced himself to me. He showed me his impressive vampire fangs, jumped to the passenger seat, and prepared to alight. After a little lunch, he would gleefully join me at my desk while I tried to work.

At this point let me give you a little background on myself. In college I had majored in English, pre-med biology, and secondary education. When I didn't go into medicine—that's a very long, disheartening story, I specialized first in English, getting a Master's Degree, then later switched to psychology. It was in psychology that I continued my studies. That gave my communications' business a broad range of resources and informational skills to offer. As a result, I did projects for pharmaceutical companies, shipboard electronics firms, and management training publishers for example.

This meant I spent a good deal of my time at home, working in my office, hunkered over my desk, researching and writing. Of course, Faust kept me company, languorously draped over the fax machine when my IBM Selectric typewriter was not available.

We had come to an understanding about my typewriter keyboard. He would not lie on it when I was typing. This was not so much out of respect for my work and that my earnings filled his tummy with cat food. It was more out of his irritation caused by the movement of my fingers on the keys underneath him as he tried to nap. And when the typewriter was not in use, I would not ask him to remove himself from it. Well, as a general rule.

This was in spite of his fur continually falling in between the keys and making me periodically have to dig it out with an unbent paper clip and vacuum cleaner upholstery attachment. If I forgot about our deal, he would get my attention by patting my cheek.

I was pleased to note that we were reaching a compromise about most things of importance. He indicated what I should do … and I did it. It was hard to argue with a being that responded to your protestations by slumping over his stomach and leisurely licking his genitals. However, for one fleeting moment, I thought I had discovered that Faust had what might be thought of as a "submissive" side. When I suggested he wear a harness and leash to go for a walk, he quietly complied—at least, I took his not balking to be compliance. What did I know?

After the fifth person stopped and commented on this not nearly-fully-furred cat that walks on a leash, stating the expected, "I didn't know cats would walk on a leash!" while he lifted his whiskers, I knew I had been hornswoggled. Submissive? Yeah, sure. He knew how great he looked in his blue harness which complimented his silver-gray fur and amber eyes. He knew his confident strut would draw people to him like a magnet. I suspected he was, as Yogi Bear said, just "smarter than the average bear."

He had spelled it out for me. Harness and leash meant going outside. Interestingly, he would not go outside without it. Maybe it was his security blanket. Wearing it meant safely exploring everywhere he wanted. He climbed trees, swinging precariously on thin branches. He jumped into the rapidly-accumulating fall leaves in the backyard, rolling on the grass and dirt. He chewed anything that used to hold chlorophyll and then vomited it up—outside when I was lucky. Wearing his livery meant being lauded by other inferior species in the front yard or along the neighborhood street. What more could he ask.

Subtlety was not his strong point. After that, he would bring his harness to me in his mouth, the leash dragging on the floor behind him, when he was sure I had done enough work. I could've fooled myself into thinking that he was trying to get me to exercise, looking out for my figure and health. But I was getting better at accepting the reality of the nuances of cat thinking and behavior. He knew what he wanted and went about getting it in whatever way was most practical. You had to admire that trait.

Unlike some other cats, he chose to come when called. However, I did not dare say, "Come" or "Come here" or "Cat" or "Here, kitty, kitty." His responding to any of that would have been kowtowing to an authority he didn't recognize. I simply called his name. No matter where he was in the house, if he heard "Faust," he came running. Well, not exactly at a gallop ... or even a race walk. That was too dog-like and eager. More precisely, it was more like a sedate trot which demonstrated his interest but nothing more for me to make assumptions about.

It was at this time that I noticed he liked to do things I asked of him. Again, it was not a matter of compliance but part of a game activity with me. If he could stimulate me to play with him more often, that suited him just fine—so much the better. I made a mental note to myself to pursue this further. His creativity seemed boundless.

If I tossed the Wiffle ball, he might race after it, pushing it along in front of himself. He might immediately get behind it and knock it back to me with his paw, like a Red Sox center-fielder throwing it back to get the runner out on third base at Fenway Park. He might athletically catch it in the air like Willie Mays. Or, he might toss it into the air himself and catch it on the fly. He was showing himself to be a cat for all seasons.

Inadvertently I discovered that he loved to chase other objects as well. Coming out of the bathroom one morning with the tie of my robe dragging on the floor, I was nearly upended when he attacked it. With his front paws he held it tight as his body curved over it, ears back, and he raked it with his back feet. As soon as I could disengage him from it, I found a piece of clothes line which I knotted at one end as a substitute. He crouched then pounced on it, flipping his body over as he hung on attacking it.

As I reeled it in, ready to toss it again, he would lower his head, curve his body to the left, and arch his back. He would raise high his tail in the shape of a question-mark and leap into the air. Ready to tell his prey who's boss, his wild inner jungle cat was making its predatory appearance. Whenever I threw the clothes line, he chased with high enthusiasm, tackling the knot, rolling from side to side, and tearing it to pieces. He threw it in front of himself and seized it again. After that, anytime he wanted to chase it, he would look at me wide-eyed with ears erect and make a chirping sound. He accompanied it by an expectant look on his raised whiskers. "You want to play with the rope?" I'd ask with equal enthusiasm. He'd seem to levitate in anticipation, shaking the front of his body in adrenaline-surging readiness.

Since Faust was becoming so gentlemanly going out, one of the first non-vet places I took him was to Lexington Gardens. I loved to go there to relax by wandering around the rows and rows of all kinds of indoor plants in containers presented on long slatted tables in the greenhouse. If I had time, I'd check out their outside plants as well.

I had a dream garden I would plant one day. It had a special design—something between formal and wild with different levels, a water feature, and boulders. I liked to imagine different perennials, annuals, grasses, shrubs, and trees in it and how they would look as the seasons changed. And maybe I would change the color scheme from time to time with the annuals: cool silver, velvety blue, or hot red and knock-your-eye-out oranges.

I wrapped Faust around my neck which was rapidly becoming his preferred travel position. From that vantage point he seemed to delight in looking down at the different color leaves, different sizes, configurations, and surfaces, from smooth to fuzzy. The heady scent of wet earth pleasantly surrounded us as water dripped from the tables onto the cement floor.

As I passed some jasmine in flower, I lifted a plant for him to sniff. He didn't seem impressed. He sneezed as if making a negative comment. But maybe his response didn't represent his reaction to all flowers. Maybe I should let him keep sniffing to see what he might like. As we approached another flowering plant, he tapped my cheek and leaned over my shoulder. I felt I should salute or at least click my heels together in response. I raised a pot to let him inhale, hoping he wouldn't decide to wrap his kitty lips around the blossom and bite it off. But he was the model of decorum, merely savoring its fragrance.

With each presentation to him he checked out African violets, begonias, nasturtiums, and cactus flowers that extended well beyond their spines. Nothing. He seemed disappointed that they didn't provide stimulation. But at least he had some success with lilies, olive, orange, lemon, freesia, and gardenia blossoms which lifted his whiskers in olfactory enjoyment.

Things were going along smoothly, with Faust on his best behavior. That is, until we reached the herb tables. My mind had wandered off again, to adding a section of edible herbs to my dream garden. As I pictured where I'd put them and how I'd set them off from the garden proper, my focus had slipped from my furry companion.

Before I could act, Faust had spotted the bite-size pots of catnip, all vibrant green and fully-leafed. In an instant he readied himself. A swan dive onto the table was imminent. He struggled to get off my shoulders. But his claws caught the fabric of my jacket. Scrambling to gain purchase, he was now hanging nearly upside down. His kitty lips puckered mere inches away from the aromatic leaves. Using karate-like moves, I tried to keep him off the table. It flashed into my mind, What if someone is watching. I looked around the greenhouse as I held onto his now-outstretched body. This was a catastrophe in the making.

I carefully detached his claws one by one, only to find other claws had snagged me in their place. He was in full gravity-enhanced downward pursuit while I was feebly attempting the equivalent of upward triceps curls with a python. Grappling, I finally managed to secure him under my arm. Cautiously I tried to raise his squirming body onto my shoulders. Did I really think this would work? Since he could still see and whiff the catnip which was transforming him into a starving tiger ready to ravage a small water buffalo.

Despite my grip, his body started to levitate. The countdown for his re-launch had begun. Downward he thrust his paws again. I caught him in mid-air by his hind quarters. Eyes wide and pupils dilated, he was swinging his front legs. If only he could swipe the hallucinogenic leaves that whispered his name. I was now panic-stricken.

Quickly kneeling on the water-drenched floor, I wrestled with him. Our limbs flying above the slatted table. With gargantuan effort I immobilized him for a moment against my chest. Without thinking, I tore off a small leaf of catnip and shoved it under his nose. He began to smack his lips, chew, drool, and writhe. Frazzled, I hoped for the best and re-placed him on my shoulders. "Stay there. We have to get out of here ASAP." The pilfered leaf had his body curling and uncurling, head lolling. I swear I could hear him moan, "Hey, man, that's great leaf."

My armpits were ringed with sweat as I put him in a kitty half-nelson with one hand and grabbed the four-inch pot of catnip from which I had stolen the leaf with the other. I stood up. My knees were drenched and pant legs dripping. I practically threw my credit card at the cashier and hurried to the car. No matter how stern and reproachful I felt, I had to let Faust continue his psychedelic trip ("Hey, mama!") someplace safe. At least on the passenger seat he was away from prying eyes.

Back home I needed to find a location that would keep the plant from being attacked before I could gradually dole out the fresh leaves to him. Where could the plant get sunshine to grow but not be available to kitty teeth. I finally hung the pot high from the curtain rod over the kitchen sink with a piece of twine. I could reach it but Faust couldn't. It worked beautifully ... for a week. That is, until Faust perfected his raw-catnip retrieval performance.

It was amazing to behold. Mesmerized, I watched him employ an Olympic-style high jump using the Western roll technique. Because he had to leap over the sink he apparently had decided against using Dick Fosbury's backwards, head-first "Fosbury Flop." Part of his challenge was to detach the plant pot which had been so well secured by twine to the rod. No problem for one with his ingenuity and athleticism. He simply brought down the plant, curtain rod, and curtains.

Looking at the broken pot and the soil-decorated sink and counters, I knew I should have foreseen this and used breakable string instead. But as a dull-witted human, I had forgotten how innovative and clever cats, especially Faust, could be. Despite the resulting minor destruction, I had to admit that it was a gold-medal-winning jump with Faust totally clearing the sink by a world's record of 3.54 centimeters. As his own reward he went on a catnip-leaf binge, saliva-soaked leaf fragments covering his glassy-eyed face. It left him flat on his back on the kitchen floor with all four legs splayed. After that the only feline marijuana he received was a pinch of dried fresh catnip, once every two days. The fruits of his labor were thereafter kept in a cat-proof container under lock and key.

CHAPTER 8

MINDING HIS ETIQUETTE
✻✻

One evening I was seated at the dining room table having my vegetarian dinner of salad greens, broccoli, cauliflower, tomatoes—drizzled with olive oil, vinegar, and herbs—and a homemade veggie burger covered in guacamole and salsa. Faust jumped up on the chair beside me, sat on his hind legs and glanced around. He looked as if he were disappointed he didn't have his own place setting and plate. He reached over and patted my arm to get my attention. As he looked up at me, his message was clear: Hey, what about me?

I retrieved a sandwich plate from the kitchen, put some of my salad greens and a little of his canned cat food on it, and placed it on the table in front of him. Since he could not quite reach the plate from a sitting position, he stood, placed his paws on either side of the plate, and began to eat ever so daintily.

Generally being a fast learner, at least when not being challenged by a cat, I put the super-thick Boston Yellow Pages phone book on his chair. Next evening he would not have to stand up at the dinner table. The next evening he then leapt on the chair, sat straight up on the phone book, and leaned forward slightly in anticipation. He used his right paw to get his food closer before nibbling it off his plate. If he had used a napkin to frequently dab his mouth, I wouldn't have been the least bit surprised.

One of the manuscripts on which I was working was about decision making for managers using a Baysian statistics formula. It was for the training arm of the American Management Association publishing company. The hypothesis was that if you applied the probability of something working to the various options available for a particular decision, you could simplify the process and make better decisions.

I knew psychologically-speaking that if you did a rational and emotional cost-benefit analysis for each option available, you could be more comfortable that the option you decided upon had less overall risk. I wondered how this formula would quantify human motivation and intention and the degree to which the decision maker was actually involved in the problem.

I thought they were missing the boat by leaving out intuition. Intuition represents what the decision maker knows but doesn't see, is not obvious, or isn't understood by reason. Patterns in body language, specific nonverbal behaviors, attitudes, beliefs, values, related emotions, present and past experiences, and associations can contribute significantly to one's decision making. Using these factors can add new awareness, new options, perspectives, and/or a different context to the problem. However, management at this time was not appreciative of using anything but rational analysis to make decisions. I definitely wasn't convinced it was the best way to make a decision. But, then again, they weren't paying me for being convinced.

Instead of mailing the next chapter (this was before e-mail with document attachments), I decided to hand-deliver it to their Waltham office. In this way I could talk with Jonas, the one who assigned me this project. I needed clarification about the types of examples and case studies he specifically wanted as well as the format of the next chapter's tests.

Waltham, which was home of the Waltham Watch Company from 1854 until 1957, was considered the prototype for 19th Century industrial planning. It was the first to produce watches on an assembly line, making over thirty-five million watches before it closed. Contributing to the labor movement and the American Industrial Revolution, it is now more a center for research and education with Brandeis

University, which focuses on liberal arts, and Bentley University, which focuses on business education.

Of course, Faust sensed I was getting ready to go out so he brought me his harness. It seemed to me that he didn't really care whether we went for a walk or took a ride. With lifted whiskers and alert ears, he indicated that he was glad to go out and do it with me, irrespective of what specifically we were going to do or where we were going to go. "Out" was the operant word. Once in the car he climbed into my lap and snuggled up, purring.

When we arrived at Jonas's office, I parked my small car in their small lot. Since I couldn't park on the end of a line, I hoped I'd still be able to avoid scratches from door scrapes on either side of me. Fat chance of that happening. I lowered all the windows about two inches for Faust on this nippy day. Before I could open the door, Faust jumped onto my shoulders and curled himself around my neck. "No, you can't come in with me. It's cool enough for you to stay in the car. I'll be right back." Faust was still not accepting of the word "no." Why not, he seemed to ask with one ear flattened to the side. He was all dressed up and ready to go. "Really. I'll be out very soon. I promise."

As I tried to slip out the car in the claustrophobically-tight space between cars, I had to repeatedly remove a clinging Faust. He was re-attaching himself to my neck like a fur scarf filled with static electricity. I firmly placed him on the driver's seat. He jumped onto my shoulder again before I could squeeze through the door. Immediately he re-curled up securely around my neck, stabbing me with his hypodermic needlelike claws which clung tightly to the flesh of my shoulders through my lightweight jacket. This was to be a battle I knew I would not win.

"Okay," I said, "but you're not going to like this." He looked at me with eyebrows raised as if to ask how I could possibly know what he would or would not like. You humans are so presumptuous. I tried to put him down on the asphalt driveway to walk in under his own power. That wasn't what he had in mind. Annoyed by his pigheadedness, I still vowed this was not going to be a big fight with him over such a trivial control issue. Especially not in a parking lot when I was concerned about being late for an appointment.

Loosening his grip, he gently kneaded my shoulders as if to soften my response to his resolve. You clever little dickens, I thought. He stayed in place on my shoulders and inspected the people on the sidewalk and in the traffic. At moments like this, I thought, perhaps it would have been more appropriate to have named him "Machiavelli." And so it goes.

As it turned out, which I hated to admit, his coming along into the office was not a half-bad idea. When I walked in, the twentyish, long-haired, redheaded receptionist, Liz, who was often somewhat formal with me, did a double-take. Apparently she had never seen a live cat collar before. This prompted her to start to ooh and ahh.

Getting up from her desk, she circled around and began petting Faust, talking baby-talk to him. She was all over him, like a bumblebee gathering pollen from a flower. Without taking her eyes off him, she asked in my direction, if he always rode on my shoulders. Faust was again in his element. He rolled and stretched his head so she could catch all the places that needed scratching. I should have known there was a method to his seemingly perverse behavior. He kneaded my shoulders. I thought, Yeah, yeah, I got it.

She reluctantly buzzed Jonas I was there and slowly went back to her desk, perhaps not wanting to be seen devoting her time to a cat rather than to typing correspondence or filing. When Jonas came out, all hustle and bustle as his title required, he stopped short. There was a lot more of him—maybe thirty pounds worth—since we had last met. "What the—?" He eyed Faust.

Even being a dyed-in-the-wool dog person, Jonas too could not resist Faust's half-closed amber eyes as they looked up at him. Faust then showed him that come-hither flash as he swished his tail languidly from side to side. Jonas melted enough to stroke Faust's head and tell him how beautiful he was. I could feel Faust smile.

In Jonas's office we discussed the next chapter. Because Faust was present and not in the car where I would have worried about the temperature despite the day's coolness, we could take a little more time for hashing out the details. Contrary to my expectation, Faust stayed perfectly still.

All the while, he sleepily took in his surroundings: Jonas's Boston College pennant, a putter in the corner, bookcase with football statue, a blue ribbon for his red setter from some dog show, a leftover half of a double-cheeseburger in the wastebasket which held his attention for a moment, and a photo of two extremely-overweight children eating chili cheese hot dogs. Their smiling faces were smeared with mustard and they each held a thirty-two-ounce sugared drink in hand.

When we finished, Jonas appreciatively commented to me, "You certainly have him well-trained." I could feel Faust's body stiffen and claws dig in deeply. "No," I answered, trying not to show the excruciating pain from his penetrating talons, "he has me well-trained." Jonas laughed at his perception of my self-deprecation. His gapping-shirt belly jiggled in cadence. Faust's body relaxed at that too. I reminded myself to later check for blood spots on my clothing as well as the date of my last tetanus vaccination. I'd also have to find him a nail clipper before he sent me to the emergency room.

As I finally slipped back into the car, Faust released his grip and slid back onto my lap, purring loudly, for the trip home. Once at home, he chirped for me to get the clothes line. I think he felt he deserved it because he had been so calm on the drive to and from Waltham. He had been so patient with Liz. And he had been supremely tolerant in his interaction with Jonas who smelled of, dare I say it, "dog." I had to admit he did show uncommon poise and appreciated etiquette in all those situations. When he was right, he was right. So I threw the clothes line and he chased it around the kitchen and living room, just short of his running out of breath

CHAPTER 9

VIEWING PREFERENCES
✳✳

In the evenings when Faust and I sat on the sofa to watch a movie, the national news, a PBS program, or some dramatic series, he would dictate what he liked and what I should watch. You could tell he liked "The Rockford Files." It had all the essential components Faust resonated to. There was James Garner's easy-going, reactive style of acting, Angel Martin's weasel-ly behavior, all the car chases, and other action. He lifted his whiskers at Garner's seemingly cowardly behavior that was inevitably followed by some clever maneuver or con game. I swear he would chuckle whenever Garner smiled and cleverly inserted some sly humor. As soon as the Mike Post – Pete Carpenter "Rockford Files" theme music came, Faust cocked his head to the left and raised his whiskers. This show was definitely on his Acceptable List.

When Nova came on, if any animals were present, he would sit below the television, enrapt, and studiously watch the action. Birds, big cats, squirrels, horses, and butterflies, especially the Monarch butterfly migration, excited him. Even snakes, crocodiles, or lizards could hold his attention for a moment or two. But dogs? They were a different story. Dogs left him not only totally disinterested but also annoyed. Those feelings seemed to me to be contradictory but apparently not to Faust.

To show his contempt for them he walked back and forth on the cabinet in front of the screen so I couldn't see anything. He did this in case I was not already aware about canines. In his estimation humans could be, to put it charitably, slow on the uptake. His goal was to let me know that these canids were creatures to be ignored. They could contaminate you, leaving you useless to cats in general and to him in particular.

Surprising to me, film noir seemed to fascinate him, especially the classic, "Double Indemnity." He would walk back and forth on the carpet below the TV and occasionally stretch himself into a standing position to look carefully at the screen. He never walked in front of the screen when it was on. Barbara Stanwyck seemed to be of particular interest. Perhaps he liked her seductive conniving or her feline way of moving. He would sometimes pat the screen when she was present.

Perhaps he interpreted the movie not to be about greed and sex but more about the characters Walter Neff and Phyllis Dietrichson's mutual need to commit a crime, each requiring the other's participation to make it work. She wanted her husband out of the way. As an insurance salesman, he wanted to commit the perfect crime, to "crook the house," as he puts it. So they worked together, unthinking about the consequences and implications of their act. I could agree with Faust on that. Even though he didn't discriminate by gender, he was less interested in MacMurray than Stanwick especially when MacMurray repeated his coldly mechanical response of "Yeah, baby," to Stanwyck. Faust wrinkled his nose as if to say, "Pfui!"

But perhaps he just liked the savvy, taut, and cynical way Billy Wilder directed this movie version of the James M. Cain's novel, one pioneering the film noir genre in the U.S. Maybe Faust was also a burgeoning movie critic, like Roger Ebert. His second favorite noir classic film was "D.O.A." with Edmond O'Brien. I had the impression he had figured out the labyrinthine threads of the sub-plots before I did, you know, like how and why Eugene Philips died, how Frank Bigelow was involved, and why it wasn't really about the shipment of iridium even though Bigelow glowed under x-ray.

Those two films were not the only films he saw and passed upon as Acceptable. In particular he seemed riveted by Frank Sinatra in "The Manchurian Candidate," standing up in front of the screen to carefully watch the often surreal-appearing action. The various action scenes and running horses in "Butch Cassidy and the Sundance Kid" appealed to him as well. He couldn't take his eyes of the screen when the escaping Butch and Sundance find themselves stopped and trapped at the edge of a cliff. Butch says "Jump!" and Sundance looks askance at him. Might as well. Together they plunge off the cliff, shouting, "Oh, shit!" Of course, he is fascinated by the big shoot-out at the end.

Stanley Kubrick's "Dr. Strangelove: Or How I Learned to Stop Worrying and Love the Bomb" held his interest but only intermittently. Mostly it was when George C. Scott was stuffing another piece of gum into his mouth and then jumping about, flailing his arms as he spouted off about Peter Bull, the Russian ambassador, being able to see the Big Board in the War Room. But he really resonated to Slim Pickens when he rode the nuclear bomb down through the bomb bay doors. But it was mostly Pickens's shouting "Whaaa hoooo!" as if riding a bucking bronco, waving his ten-gallon cowboy hat, that intrigued Faust the most. He even did a little shuffle jig-like dance in front of the screen as the bomb disappears into the distance.

But of all the films he liked, I suspect his all-time, favorite had to be "Young Frankenstein." Despite Faust's serious adherence to his no-nonsense Cat Code of Royal Behavior, he invariably stared at the screen. Cocking his head to the right side, he twitched his tail and jumped about as the Creature and Dr. Frankenstein did their sterling performance of a Busby Berkeley in "Putting on the Ritz." There was no doubt he loved all the clever insanity of the Mel Brooks' film.

CHAPTER 10

CONSTRUCTING A CAT TREE
✼✼

Now that Faust had been with me for several months, like a good kitty mom I had ordered a large cat tree. It was to be delivered that afternoon by United Parcel Service. Around three o'clock the delivery person dressed in his brown uniform lugged the large, heavy box to the door. I was surprised. I expected to receive a fully-assembled tree, like the ones I had seen in PetSmart. I thought that's what I had ordered. Faust stood on the back of the upholstered chair near the front window and peered out at him.

I had thought Faust might come to the door out of curiosity. After all, I was there to protect him if he was afraid. I soon discovered, however, he didn't answer doors, but not out of fear. Answering doors was what humans did. Good grief! It was what dogs did! Cats did *not* answer doors. Sometimes I felt like a little developmentally disabled learner.

The five-foot-long, heavy cardboard carton was glued together at the sides and had numerous industrial-strength, large copper staples at the opening ends for good measure. Using pliers and a slot-head screwdriver, I twisted, pushed, and pulled, grunting all the while, face red. I finally managed to get the ends open. There was no way on earth, however, I could open it at the sides without a sturdy utility knife or bulging biceps, like Sylvester Stallone's in "Rocky."

I tried pulling the carpet-covered thick wooden disassembled pieces from the box but they wouldn't budge. They were wedged in even more closely than commuters on the morning MBTA (or Massachusetts Bay Transit Authority) green-line to Boston. However, being as obstinate as the box seemed to be, I swore I would do this no matter what it took.

Faust was entranced with this mysterious enclosure. He tried to squeeze into the end where I was yanking. "No, no, Faust. Let me pull it out for you. No. You're in the way. Watch out. You're going to get squished. Damn it, Faust! Let me do this by myself!"

Taking extreme umbrage at my speaking to him in such harsh tones, he retired to the other end of the box. There he tried to squeeze his body inside it as well. I rousted him from the box then tried to elevate that end so gravity might lend a hand. Just as things began to shift in the right direction,

Faust raced to the end where movement was occurring. He attacked the protruding piece with glee.

I laid down the end I was holding and spoke pseudo-enthusiastically to him through my clenched teeth, "Faust, how would you like a yummy kitty treat? Maybe some Friskies' Treats?" His ears rose into an alert position and he trotted into the kitchen where I gave him enough treats to stuff a squab. Maybe, I thought, this way I could make a little progress before he returned to render his overly energetic assistance.

By fits and starts, and lots of swearing, I did get the large pieces of lumber out of the box. Whew! The actual setting up of the tree, however, required my screwing heavy squat pieces of carpet-covered lumber with screw projections into other similar with washers and holes. At that point my only hope was that the result was going to be both secure and tree-like. The instructions had provided some options for arrangement of the pieces so I went for the most intriguing structure I could imagine.

Placement of this tall massive construction had all the earmarks of a problem. I needed to find a location where Faust could not jump onto anything else from it. He had already checked out the bookcase's built-in shelves and the mantelpiece where he tiptoed around pieces of art I had placed there. I needed a place where his climbing up and down would not put him or my furnishings at risk.

Completed, the tree was huge, heavy, and tippy. Fortunately, the designer had given that some thought. They had included a spring-loaded, two-piece metal pole with a rubber tip on one end. You would screw the other end into the top of the tree and place the metal-reinforced rubber tip against the ceiling in order to make the unit more stable. There appeared to be only one good location. By the window overlooking the backyard would give him access to several things: sunshine, a clear view of birds in the feeder hanging from the roof soffit. And he could longingly watch the squirrels as they scrambled up and down the dogwood tree nearest the house.

I awkwardly dragged the weighty sculpture inch by inch across the living room. In trying to keep it upright as it caught on the carpet, I strained my lower back and twanged my sciatic nerve. I also got more than my share of carpet fuzz from it in my mouth, on my face, and in my hair as it periodically banged against my skull.

But, it was an admirable-looking kitty tree. It was grey and white with a tight, Berber-like carpet pile. Hopefully this style carpet would shed less ... well, a *little* less than some other less-tight piles. At its hefty price it had better be better. Even though

Faust had been so eager to attack and play with it in its embryonic form, he showed no immediate interest after it was constructed and in place. "Well, crap!" I sighed. That was a bit discouraging.

Like most cats, Faust had a tendency not to appear predictable. Dogs were predictable; cats weren't. It was an image thing. As I massaged my aching lower back, feeling momentarily abused by such an ungrateful cat, he ran toward the tree. At full tilt he scaled its heights. Then in the circular crow's nest at the top, he promptly fell asleep. With a smile, I whispered in his direction, "I'm sorry I misjudged you. Enjoy!"

Before I could throw away the long box later that day, Faust made it clear by crawling inside it that this likewise was his. In his first weeks with me we didn't do much playing. In contrast, he was now ready for just about anything, wheezing or not. I rolled the Wiffle ball into the long box. Faust went after it with all the intensity of a female lion going after a gazelle to feed her cubs.

I could hear him batting it about in there. Then suddenly out flew the ball with Faust racing after it, batting it ahead of himself as he met it. He energetically hit it all around the living room and kitchen ... until his lungs put a halt to it. Suddenly he fell to the floor, lay on his side, gasping for breath. Dr. Katuna had said to be aware of that. I had to let him regain his breath then re-direct his activities to something less taxing. Sounding simple, it wasn't.

That was the first I had encountered the gritty, full-blown reality of his pulmonary problem. Yes, he wheezed but he was recovering so well from all his other medical conditions that I let his fibrotic lungs and their oxygen deficiency slip out of my awareness. More guilt. I would have to find ways to play with him that were fun but a little less strenuous. Or that were strenuous for a shorter period of time. No more full-out chasing prey.

When I had asked Dr. Katuna about emergency treatments for his lungs, I had had no idea what his oxygen deficiency would look like. The answer was, "Nothing." Unfortunately cats couldn't wrap their lips around an inhaler, exhale on cue, and then inhale the corticosteroid when the plunger was pushed. Besides available inhalers were designed for critters that were at least twenty times Faust's weight.

Fortunately for other cats with similar airway inflammation, years later an aerosol inhaler was developed especially for the one-in-five feline asthma sufferers. So, instead of wrapping their lips around a small tube, the cats breathe into a clear plastic mask. The bronchodilator is delivered passively to their lungs to not only reduce inflammation but also increase their ability to breathe.

At this moment I raced to his side, stroked his head and down his back. "It's okay, Faust. You're just a little winded from your spectacular sports performance. Just relax. I hear the Sox will be contacting you for their team. Relax, baby cat. It will be okay soon. You just overdid it a little. Even professional sports stars do that. You're such a good boy. You're Mommy's boy. Relax and breathe slowly. Mom is here." At least I wasn't talking baby-talk to him. After about seven minutes he began to stir and try to get up. In another four minutes he was on his feet looking for the Wiffle ball.

This experience left me very conflicted. He had a severe health problem and his activity needed to be controlled to some degree. But, at the same time, it was important that I not think of him or treat him as a "disabled" cat. I didn't want to become overly protective of him. I didn't want to restrict his play so he might never gasp for air. He needed a chance to enjoy his new life ... as did I. It made me sigh with regret. I wanted a clear-cut answer ... but there was none. I'd have to take it day by day, with me keeping his breathing problem in the back, *not* the front, of my mind. I had to make sure he would still enjoy the Wiffle ball and his clothes line.

CHAPTER 11

DOING ROCKPORT
✳✳

On Thursday I completed as much of my work as I could on the next decision making chapter and on my other projects. I wanted Faust and me to have our Friday free for a trip. I thought he might enjoy Rockport. Rockport, with its boulder-strewn beaches and prominent fishing harbor, especially for lobster, is a vacation spot and tourist town located approximately thirty-five miles northeast of Boston.

At the tip of the Cape Ann peninsula, it is directly east of Gloucester and surrounded on three sides by the Atlantic Ocean. At one time the quarries of Rockport were the major source of high-grade granite. But when concrete replaced granite in construction, Rockport became first an artists' colony, then vacation home of the well-to-do, and finally a permanent tourist magnet.

Faust was in his harness and the car had its supply of bottles of water, his water dish, dry cat food, litter pan on the back floor, apples, and peanut butter granola bars I had thrown together. Of course, his carrier graced the back seat as well. It looked as if we were ready to leave. In the event he chose not to walk on his leash or hang around my neck, I also had a knapsack with a padded bottom I would wear. That meant he could ride in the open on my back allowing him to look around at all the new sights. I took a broad-brimmed straw hat to keep the sun off him, if he didn't walk, and off me.

We were off by nine o'clock following Route 128 north to Gloucester and Rockport and to Route 127. Faust sat on my lap and watched everything that whizzed by us. Once in Rockport we discovered that while there was metered parking in town, we could park for free at the Blue Gate Parking Lot which was about three-quarters of a mile from town. We would have to walk to and from it but we wouldn't have the inconvenience of returning to feed a meter every hour. There was a trolley that ran between the lot and town but Faust gave it a thumb's down for being too claustrophobic. Humans were all crowded together and some of them had—dare I utter the word—dogs.

There was so much to see. What had been quaint fisherman and lobsterman shacks had been recycled into restaurants, galleries, shops, and tourist attractions with that same rustic ambiance. Faust quickly decided he did not want to walk because, as he indicated by hopping from one foot to the other, the asphalt and then the sidewalks were hot. But I suspected it was really because there were more people wandering around than he had anticipated. I put him around my neck under the brim of my hat and that seemed to satisfy him ... at least for the moment.

Men, women, and children ooh-ed and ahh-ed at Faust, asking his name and did he always ride like that? They stated the expected, "I didn't know cats did that," but he received less attention than he expected he would be given the number of people milling around. Sadly for him, he was not the only animal being carried on tour. There were plenty of little dogs being ferried around and larger dogs on leads. At least there were very few cats.

We entered nearly every shop or gallery we encountered, marveling at the range of goods and art forms. But when the proprietor inevitably spotted Faust lurking under my brim, I had to convince her or him that he was well-behaved and not going to disrupt anything. The proprietors seemed more obliging than they might have been in Boston, particularly in the galleries on Newbury Street where animal were *verboten*. Still their reluctance was palpable.

The range of art was spectacular: wood carvings of shore birds, bronze sculptures, hand-woven fabrics, and representational and abstract paintings in oils, water colors, acrylics, and pastels. Of course, most of it reflected the beautiful old, red fishing buildings around the harbor, boats moored in the water, and seascapes which revealed the subtle color changes in the sea and sky at different times of the day and under different weather conditions. It was easy to see why people liked living in Rockport.

It was lunch time and both of us had noisy stomachs. We looked for some place with the appropriate ambiance to eat—we definitely didn't want any fast food. We stopped at a fish restaurant that had outside dining as well. A tanned young woman with long dark hair approached to wait on us. Her name tag said "Laurie," and she gushed all over Faust. "I just love cats!" she exclaimed with more enthusiasm than Faust wanted to hear. "Could I hold him?" Faust was not particularly interested in letting strangers handle him. He let her know as gently as possibly the answer by tucking his nose under his paw closest to my throat.

Fortunately his action registered with her so I didn't have to say anything. Instead, continuing to stroke his back, she asked if she could bring him a complimentary saucer of milk with our meal. He seemed to feel that was an appropriate response and lifted his whiskers at her. She giggled, scratched him under the chin, and rubbed her face against his. Faust wasn't quite sure what to make of that so he cocked an ear at her. She smiled and hurriedly sent our order on to the cook.

We dined *al fresco* at a café table with metal chairs on broiled bluefish and a variety of salad greens which we shared, and his milk, which we did not share. Laurie had thoughtfully, perceptively brought two dinner plates along with his saucer of milk. This allowed me to apportion the fish and greens. As he stood on his own chair to reach he plate, he ate with Emily Post's approval.

He nibbled slowly and carefully from his dish, his paws on the edge of the table. People walking by the restaurant stopped and stared, incredulous. They pointed and chuckled about Faust's formal table manners. Invariably, numbers of people would ask, "Does he do this all the time?" Others begged me to allow them to take a photograph because no one was going to believe them about this cat back home.

As we finished our meal and his public attention had momentarily waned, we hastened to the beach. The scent of seaweed and the salt water breezes were refreshing. I took off my shoes to let the sand sift through my toes. But Faust was not sure he liked the deep sand. It seemed he was walking one step back for every two forward. Besides, the sand was getting caught in the webbing between his toes.

With every step he took he melodramatically shook each paw in succession, pausing only to make practical use of the sand since it was convenient. Besides, it covered better than dirt in his backyard did. When we approached the water's edge, his reaction to the wet sand was not at all what I had expected.

No sooner had I put him down on it, than he ran along the water's edge, dodging the small waves, chasing sandpipers, and pulling me along behind on his leash. He even ruffled the feathers of a large, imperious-looking seagull that had lighted for a moment at the water's edge to search for tiny crabs.

Incredibly Faust seemed in his element. He was running and leaping into the air. To my astonishment, he even did a back flip, something which I had never seen before, much less thought possible. Now why couldn't I have caught that on film, I sighed, disgruntled. I hadn't brought a camera because that would have been too much to handle with Faust.

With his whiskers raised as if inhaling a new, re-invigorated life, he was a portrait of primitive, natural feline joy. He was expressing his inner tiger. It was then I began to gently pull back on his leash, feeling guilty I had to curtail his *joie de vivre* at being wild and free.

Before we left, we visited the Paper House on Pigeon Hill Street, an architectural wonder. It consists of two rooms of furniture either constructed of rolled newspaper or covered with newspaper. Even the walls were made from newspaper. Tapping my cheek with his paw, Faust told me he was wearying of this. It looked to him like a big weather protection headache ... and what if uncouth dogs lifted a leg on it? Newspaper was not practical for anything than his kitty pan. So we headed back to the car.

On the drive back home he slept, snuggled on my lap, no longer interested in the scenery. We arrived at the house in time for his dinner and the McNeil-Lehrer News Hour. I was tired. I chomped on an apple and a peanut butter granola bar I had taken with us. A large glass of lemon water helped dislodged it and go down.

It was too early to go to bed and too late to watch a movie. I curled up on the deep-cushioned sofa where Faust joined me. I was going to read P.D. James' *Adam Dalgliesh mystery, Cover Her Face.* I liked how James so carefully delineated the location of each story such that the setting of the book became a character as well.

Faust had other ideas about what I should be doing, like brushing him.

His brush lay on the end table next to where I was sitting so he leaned across me and batted it toward me in case I had not read his mind. I didn't catch on right away so he patted my cheek to get my attention. After a long day of sea and sand, he indicated he needed a strenuous grooming.

Settling sphinx-like on the cushion beside me, he waited with anticipation. The moment the bristles met his fur, he stretched sensuously to show me every hair and square centimeter of skin to be brushed. I focused on the area above his tail. Suddenly his haunches and tail went straight up. His eyes squinted to tiny, evil-looking slits. His flat, rough pink tongue flicked like a rattler's as if to catch the scent of a rodent passing by. Next he began lifting one hind foot than the other, as if he were in the groove dancing to some hot French Quarter jazz band.

Apparently I had found the ultimate itch that begged to be scratched—one he couldn't reach. I was practically strangling myself as I tried hard to refrain from laughing out loud. The last thing I wanted to do was insult his Martha Graham—or was it Alvin Ailey—interpretive performance. It would have been great video content. I had to make a note to get a video camera.

When I stopped, he stopped. He rolled over, revealing his partially-white tummy, begging me to brush him there too. Some cats want their tummies rubbed or brushed but respond with fear when you try. They can sink meat-tearing fangs into the flesh of your arm. If Faust panicked, his fangs could have done a real number on me.

Faust, however, responded by writhing as I moved the brush from under his jaw, down his chest, and toward his groin area. He raised each of his front paws in turn so I could do his armpits as well. He spread his back legs to enable me to run the brush over his inner thighs, rolling right then left so I could include the sides of his belly. When he decided he had had enough, he leaned forward and softly nipped my hand. The sofa cushions and I were covered in gray and white hair. The brush was clogged with it. Fur decorated the lining of my nose, the corners of my mouth, my cheeks, my glasses, and somehow had insinuated itself inside my blouse as well.

As soon as he regained his royal composure, he separated himself from me on the sofa to proceed to lick his entire body. Perhaps he was simply showing the re-establishment of his feline independence and control. Or ... perhaps he was ridding himself of any human odor, specifically my odor. No, I didn't want to think that. I preferred to give him the benefit of the doubt by choosing the more acceptable, explanation.

CHAPTER 12

EXERCISING WITH MOM
✶✶

Before I encountered Faust, I used to run several miles every morning, doing forty miles a week. Since he didn't want to be left behind, especially in the morning at our breakfast time together, I had to figure out how I could take him with me. Even if he chose to, he physically couldn't run on his leash beside me—not for any distance. Putting him in his knapsack would bounce him around on my back, perhaps getting him dizzy or nauseous as well as messing up my stride. There was no easy way to take him on a run with me. I had to come up with another idea so we could share that time together.

In the garage I had a very old Raleigh girl's bike to which was attached a rectangular wire basket. It occurred to me that perhaps I could pad the basket, put him in, and secure his harness in some way to it so he couldn't fall or jump out. That seemed more than a little iffy, maybe even a little dangerous. Still, I wondered if it might be worth a trial run. Faust always seemed to be up for almost anything. After all, I had seen little dogs riding that way ... and as Faust had kept reminding me, he was infinitely smarter than any of them. Of course, I was a tad prejudiced in his direction.

After dusting off the bike and putting a towel in the basket, I slipped Faust into his harness then secured him to the basket with his leash and fasteners. I slowly rolled the bicycle out of the garage to the driveway. Faust already seemed uncertain. Then suddenly he frantically exploded. Full of fear, he began pulling back against the harness and the toggles tethering him to the basket. He twisted and turned frenetically. He struggled mightily to free himself. My normally sedate traveling companion was nearly asphyxiating himself as he tried to get loose and out of that basket. Cold realization smacked me in the back of my head. Good grief! What had I done?

Standing over the upright bicycle frame in front of the seat, I fought with Faust to calm him as I tried to help get him loose. His paws still flailed as he continued to slip inch-by-inch from his confines. In a fury of full-pitched panic he made it crystal clear that he would not be put in such a dangerous position ever again. Neither would he be held captive in any way. He couldn't seem to believe I was so humanly stupid.

It flashed through my mind that in his current emotional state he might slip out of my hands to run down the street, dragging his leash—and perhaps the bicycle—to be hit by a car, caught by a dog, or become a homeless cat again. I couldn't allow myself to panic as well. I had to get him out of his emotional auto-pilot. If I could do that, I could quickly and safely release him.

This meant I had to interrupt his perception of the situation and get him focused on me. Constantly talking softly to him, reassuring him, incrementally holding him less firmly, I could feel him begin to relax as I unhooked him. Once I had him loose with my hands around him, he did not leap out of the basket onto the ground.

I thought if I had been in his position with some crazy giant hunkered over me, I might well have done precisely that. Instead, he glared at me for a full minute, panting. I could see he was considering all the options available to him on how he could reprimand me so I wouldn't do something so incredibly moronic ever again.

Without a clue as to what was about to happen, I felt him leave my hands. Now I panicked ... immediately envisioning him running away. But, instead, he landed on my shoulders, his claws bared, body taut, wrapping himself around my neck. "Owwww! That really hurts. Is that my punishment? Okay, I'm so sorry I frightened you. Really I am. I know that was a dumb thing to do. You have every right to be angry with me." He relaxed imperceptibly for a moment. "Okay, so what do you want me to do now? Do you want me to take you back inside? Do you want to take a walk?" I waited for a sign. His body relaxed some more. "Would you possibly want to try to take a ride anyway? I mean without your harness being secured? You could sit in the basket?"

His claws tightened on my muscles. I knew I was saying too much and saying it too fast. It was a barrage of words that he didn't understand anyway. He was a cat. I was also giving him too much to think about and probably confusing him. I paused to let it sink in. "Or ...," I resumed more slowly, thinking aloud, "if you prefer, you can stay perched right where you are. Would you like that?" A minute passed and his claws relaxed slightly. "So we'll give that a try?" I waited for some sign of disagreement.

When it didn't occur, I said with trepidation, "Okay, hang on." Slowly I balanced on the pedals, sat down on the seat, and let the bicycle roll into the street. He didn't move. I pedaled slowly at first then gradually sped up. He didn't move. If he were afraid, I knew now with every fiber of my being he would let me know in no uncertain terms. He was not bashful about expressing himself about such things, using every part of his body to let me know if necessary.

We rode around the neighborhood. Little kids on their tricycles saw us and pointed. Adults in their yards with lawnmowers at the ready laughed as we cruised by. I waved ceremoniously to them all and Faust raised his head in royal recognition. It was a given that it wouldn't be long before our daily excursions made him a neighborhood celebrity. As we later headed back up our drive, little kids were waving at their new furry friend who rode a bicycle.

Faust waited until I opened the door to the house then gingerly alighted. He was obviously no worse for wear. Of course, I couldn't say the same for my shoulders. However, he was still not pleased about what had transpired earlier. His looking up at me through half-closed eyes indicated clearly that I should always ask his preferences or permission before considering involving him in anything so risky or dangerous. He was a natural athlete with an inclination to take some risks but he was by no means an Evel Knievel. His idea of fun and adventure was not attempting to jump over the Snake River in Twin Falls, Idaho, only to crash a few feet from the river's edge.

I felt humbled by my disregard for him. If I had only asked him what he wanted to do by putting him in the basket unlashed then watching his response to being tethered, we would not have had to go through that knock-down-drag-out fight in the basket. As much as it irked me, he was right. I had handled it badly. I sincerely apologized one more time, this time for not having asked about his wishes. It was all about respect and I'd have to remember that.

He made a big display of sniffing in my direction then sat by himself on the sofa for a while to emphasize the importance of the point he'd made. I joined him on the other end and picked up my book to read. Then as if nothing negative had occurred between us, he crawled into my lap and up against my chest, his paws on either side of my neck and burrowed his head in my chest. Of course, I had to put my book down to direct all my attention to him. He was no dummy.

He began to purr and purr loudly as I stroked his back. I hadn't heard this full, rumbling sound before. Loud, more than twenty–to–fifty Hertz, he reminded me of a 1963 Ford with a hole in its muffler. I took his cuddling as a sign he'd keep me around for a while in spite of everything I had done earlier. At least I was good at whipping that clothes line across the floor and from room to room. Soon thereafter we had our breakfast. Bicycling together became our morning exercise ritual which we continued even on drizzly days, for which I had to construct a black rain cape for him. We kept it up religiously until the first snow fall. As a result, we, I should say Faust, became famous, and maybe even a little infamous, in our neighborhood.

CHAPTER 13

EXPANDING HIS REPERTOIRE
✳✳

When we played, Faust introduced a number of interesting, new behaviors that I thought he might want to elaborate upon at some point. When I'd toss the Wiffle ball across the floor, he would run after it, tackle it, then roll over with it. I wondered what he'd do if I took the Wiffle ball and passed it over his upper body from side to side. As I did it, he rolled from side to side. I did it again but this time I snapped my fingers and said, "Good roll over" as he finished it. Hmmm, I thought, this has the makings of his doing a roll-over behavior on cue. "You're so clever," I petted him on his head.

From time to time there were other such interesting things that he enjoyed doing that seemed to indicate a potential for demonstrating what I thought of as some "human-like" athletic behaviors. I'm sure he would have been chagrinned at my labeling them as such. After all, who was I to define what was "human" and what was "cat"? I was going to have to get myself a clicker so I wouldn't have to try snapping my fingers all the time. I have never been the world's best finger snapper.

Maybe I had a show business cat in the making. He was definitely someone more talented than Morris who only sat and looked into the camera with a sulky-sounding human voiceover. Faust had imagination and creativity. I suspected he could do almost anything he chose to if he thought it was fun.

I had images of myself as a cat stage mother. Then I had to laugh to myself, No, not me. I couldn't pressure him to do anything he didn't want to do. He did it because it was a game. Once it ceased to intrigue or stimulate him, he was done with it. You can't force a cat to willingly do anything it chooses not to do because he doesn't see a benefit for him. You had to respect that. I suspect that that was one of the things Faust saw as a primary and valuable difference between cats and dogs.

Something I had to re-discover and keep foremost in my mind was that cats do not perceive time as we humans do. Humans expect other creatures, human and non-human alike, to respond immediately to anything they say and do. Cats, however, work on a slower timetable.

Time and again I've seen humans ask a cat if it wanted to go outside as the cat, looking interested in doing so, stood by the door. When the cat didn't snap-to with an expected rush on through, the human, frustrated and muttering something about the "stupid" cat, impatiently closed the door.

For cats there is no reason in non-hunting or non-emergency situations to make and act on rapid decisions. Life for them is not desperately controlled by time as it is for us humans. I wonder if they know how lucky they are not to be hurry-up-and-wait, frustrated humans.

Interestingly their more laid back approach is often associated with their sleeping sixteen hours a day. However, a good portion of that time is not in deep sleep, what humans experience in REM sleep. It is in actuality a catnap or stand-by mode. This is a very light sleep where they can switch immediately to alert mode when necessary. It's sort of like keeping their engine at idle. It's easy to see the difference between the floppy, seemingly boneless cat which is deep sleeping and the hyper-alert cat which is only napping and responds to any stimulation immediately.

Once I recognized this difference in time importance and perception, I gave Faust a little more time to decide what he wanted to do. And lo and behold, he made his decisions. Ironically, it was my accommodating to his sense of time that forced me to slow down. Over time I was able to eliminate some of that time-induced pressure on myself which had created a lot of stress for me. It has been a great relief to let it go.

On Saturday mornings we faithfully watched Crockett's Victory Garden on WGBH after our ride. Being an inveterate gardener, I lusted for a place wherein I could have both a flower and veggie garden. The rental house had landscape plantings but I felt queasy about tearing up part of the grassed yard for tomatoes, zucchini, kale, banana peppers, cucumbers, and a variety of herbs, like basil, parsley, chives, dill, tarragon, and lemon thyme. However, if I bought twenty-gallon flower pots, I could grow at least some of the veggies and herbs in them. That would be a reasonable alternative.

But that was not the only thing after which I lusted from the show. I wanted the unusual musical instrument that played the upbeat, dance-like theme song for the program. It was stringed but was struck with hammers of some sort. It was played percussively like a piano but without that piano sound.

On this particular Saturday I remembered to closely watch as the credits rolled by, pencil in hand, until the song title appeared. It was the "Gaspé Reel" played by Bill Spence and the Fennig All-Stars. Okay, great. But ... what was the instrument?

Drat! I was going to have to do some research: call WGBH, go to a music shop, go to the library to look in the *Guide to Periodical Literature* for Bill Spence, Victory Garden, "Gaspé Reel," and the Fennig All-Stars. At least I had something to go on now. My juices were really flowing about getting my hands on one of those "whatever it was."

How satisfying it is when your research pays off. After checking all of the above, I found it. Well, at least I found the name of it. It was a dulcimer, but not the delicate, hourglass-shaped, fretted instrument in the zither family that has three or four strings and is plucked or strummed on one's lap. That's called an Appalachian dulcimer (aka mountain dulcimer). Instead it was a large, many-stringed instrument with a treble and bass bridge and tuning pins on a trapezoidal sound box. Moreover, it was generally played with two small, curved, thin mallets and set at a thirty–to–forty-five degree angle on a stand when played.

Related to both the psaltery and piano, it dated back to around 900 A.D. Some version of it existed in almost every country, like the *hackbrett* in Germany, *cymbalon* in Hungary, the *santür* in India, and the *lumberjack's piano* in the Northwest of the U.S. To my surprise, Henry Ford in the 1920s had had an orchestra in Dearborn, Michigan, composed of nothing but hammered dulcimers. It was said he had done it in an effort to undermine jazz which he disliked and was determined to squelch.

When I saw a picture of it, I suddenly recalled having actually seen one played years ago in the pilot episode of Raymond Burr's "Ironside" television series in 1967. At that time I had not known what the intriguing instrument was but was not particularly impressed by how a person played it, totally without personality or melody. Having died out in popularity sometime in the early 20th Century, it was coming back great guns, especially in folk and Celtic music. I would have to see how I could find a maker or seller to acquire one. That meant more research.

With all our practice/play, Faust was getting quite proficient at rolling over on cue and jumping onto my shoulders on cue. Sometimes he would do a head-over-tail somersault. Occasionally he would stand up on his hind legs for a second or two to get my attention. That sparked the question in my mind as to whether he might be influenced to walk a distance, like across the room, on his hind legs. At that time I had finished the decision making for managers' project and was almost finished with the first-level supervisor course. I had not as yet received a self-esteem therapy manuscript by a Massachusetts writer for editing. So I used the little down time I had to work—Oops! Sorry, "play"—with Faust. I really had to be careful how I thought about our sessions together. How I defined them affected how I acted. That, in turn, affected how Faust responded.

CHAPTER 14

TRIPPING THE LIGHT FANTASTIC

✷✷

To see if I could get him to want to walk on his hind legs I first had to get him to stand, then click, praise, and reward him when he did it. It was all a game to Faust so he enthusiastically participated. He loved trying and learning new things and then demonstrating them to me. It was like, "Look at me, Mom! Look what I can do!" He looked so pleased with himself. I always gushed all over him, "What a good boy, Faust. You're such a clever cat!"

Once he would stand on cue, the challenge was to get him to take a step on cue. Treats helped. Take a step, get a treat. Take two steps, get a treat. He didn't seem to mind that the number of treats didn't increase with the number of steps he took. My goal was to encourage him by clicking, praising, and rewarding to ultimately get him to walk across the living room on his hind legs.

I caught myself getting so involved in the process that I didn't notice what he was doing all on his own. Suddenly he was adding his own personal touches: an extra step here and a flourish there. I had never thought about cats in that way. But, then again, we humans tend to think we're the only ingenious, creative critters on the planet. We tend to see animals from the smallest to the largest as simply responding automatically to situations that seriously affect their lives—a sort of simple stimulus-response, like a reflex. Faust was demonstrating to me how narrow and chauvinistic my view was. He didn't need his professor to push him to do more and different things. He was accomplishing an enormous amount all on his own. That said a great deal more about his motivation than it did about my teaching.

For fun, while he was walking several steps, I made a circular motion around him with my hand. He quickly showed me who was in charge of these sessions. He walked in a circle as if waltzing to the Blue Danube. Grudgingly, I clicked the clicker, praised, and rewarded him. However, I thought he didn't have be such a show-off about doing it perfectly on his first try. As I was soon to find out, this was not a one-time behavior. I also discovered that if I lowered my hand as I circled it around him, he would bow slightly as he did his circle. He was communicating to me that if I cared enough to stimulate him with fun things to do, he cared enough to show me he could and would follow my lead, enjoying himself in the process.

After dinner one evening as I was sitting on the sofa reading P.D. James, Faust sauntered in, sat in front of me on the carpet, and tapped me on the foot with his front paw. When he was sure he had my attention, he stood up on his hind legs, walked a few steps and made his circle. My jaw and the book dropped simultaneously in absolute astonishment. The noise of the book sliding to the floor with a resounding slap sent him onto my lap, up against my chest, licking my neck and face with his tongue. I was beginning to wonder: Was he really a cat ... or a dog in a cat suit? I had never interacted with a cat this way before. But, I suspected, that said more about me than about the interests and talents of my other cats. What sorts of things could they have done if I had encouraged them to try new behaviors? If only I had been more aware before. At least I had a leg up now.

"Good boy, Faust," I cooed and stroked his back. "Good boy. I am so proud of you. You know, no one would ever believe you did this." He snuggled against me, kneaded my stomach, climbed onto my shoulders, and fell asleep. He was obviously extremely satisfied with himself. He had every right to be. After that he finally crossed the room on his hind legs, on cue. In addition, he began to waltz whenever I circled my hand, and dipping on cue as well. I was going to have to play some Strauss waltzes to see if he could waltz to the music. I wondered if we could waltz together. But that was asking a lot ... given our differences in height.

CHAPTER 15

TRICKING OR TREATING
✶✶

The temperatures were dropping precipitously. The remaining colorful leaves were giving out their last gasp as the rays of light and cold changed their role of energy-making photosynthesis. Becoming enfeebled, they were less able to continue to grasp onto the tree branches, sadly letting go, leaving the trees bare and skeletal. Late October was approaching. As Faust and I cycled around the neighborhood, his younger fans called out to him, "Faust, are you going trick or treating?" Up until that moment, I hadn't thought about All Hallow's Eve at all, much less about whether Faust would dress up and visit the children. Good question. I had to see what Faust thought about it, although I already had a pretty good idea.

Cats are by preference nudists. They wear their fur ... period ... and that's how they like it. So dressing up tends not to be one of their "oh, boy" favorite activities. Besides, if asked, they would tell you that there are lots of provisos for any animals being dressed up. For example, they had to be able to see, hear, and breathe. If they had whiskers and/or a tail, the costume could not interfere with them. Moreover, the costume could not restrict with their movement in any way. And, if they had to wear what humans seemed to think was "cute" or "funny," they should not be left outside alone so attired. It was too dangerous. Just wearing something besides their own fur could take their mind off traffic and run out into the street. Besides, children might grab at their clothing, scare them, or hurt them.

No, I decided I wouldn't take Faust around. But I would check with him to see if he'd be interested in wearing some personality-approved costume to greet the kids who came by the house trick-or-treating. For example, would he wear his rain cape indoors? If I made a black mask of soft cotton with large eye holes that didn't intrude on his eyes, ears, or whiskers, would he wear it? He would look more like Zorro than Bela Lugosi as Dracula, but the little kids wouldn't notice or much care. Then would he lie on my shoulders? Or could I tempt him to sit in a large, orange plastic jack-o'-lantern?

Over the next ten days, I fashioned different versions of the mask for him. He wasn't opposed to it but, then again, didn't seem particularly thrilled to wear it for long.

Perhaps he'd condescend to wear it long enough to greet the trick-or-treaters. So the costume was taken care of. Now I'd have to find a plastic pumpkin to fit Faust's body. He was no longer skin and bones. It occurred to me I might have to resort to a real pumpkin which I hollowed out and lined with plastic. But that would be a sticky mess and sure to get on his fur and harden, refusing to be washed off. It sounded too yucky.

The fates must have been with me for when I stopped at a nearby Goodwill store, there in the toy area was a ratty-looking plastic pumpkin just Faust's size. Ah, things were shaping up. Rather than give out candy, I had decided to give out apples, air-popped popcorn in plastic sandwich bags, granola bars, and dried fruit roll-ups. At a party store I found two diaphanous ghosts to hang on either side of the front door lights and an acceptable vampire to hang on the front door. However, while its fangs were worthy, they paled in comparison to Faust's.

Faust had been readied at five o'clock in case children came by early, but they didn't. He was getting antsy. He had on his harness which was all right. However, the cape was getting warm. I had designed it to resist rain so it didn't breathe. By six he was ready to run to climb his tree, have something to nosh, or take a nap. But the children would expect to see him. What would I do if they didn't start coming soon?

The doorbell rang. Suddenly Faust was on his best behavior, perched in his plastic pumpkin, his mask and cape in place. I opened the door to find nearly the whole junior-sized neighborhood on the stoop. I rested the pumpkin on a kitchen stool by the front door and held a large basket full of non-candy goodies in the other.

"Look at Faust!" squealed Timmy, Jennifer, and Edward almost simultaneously, pointing. At that moment I turned to look at Faust. He was sitting up straight on his back haunches, waving his right paw at them, showing his fangs. Where did he learn to do that? They started to giggle. The giggle became a loud laugh as the others saw him and joined in. Now what, I wondered. As I looked down, I saw his long, gray tail was sticking through the cut-out for the pumpkin's nose. It was flicking at them, something like a semaphore or startled rattlesnake.

I told them to take whatever they wanted which they did. Each in turn petted Faust after doing so. This was the first time they had had the opportunity to come really close to him. Incredibly, he sat still for the seeming hordes of kids coming at him. And I suddenly realized he was actually sitting at the door "greeting" people which he indicated to me he would never lower himself to do. But maybe he did it for the children. He kept up his end like a real trouper. That is, until the last straggler had wandered by and was gone. When I closed the door, he leapt clear of the pumpkin, tore off his mask with his two paws. Looking directly at me, he then waited patiently for me to remove his cape, harness, and leash. It was obvious from his demeanor he felt he deserved a real reward. I couldn't disagree.

I had made a pumpkin pie from scratch earlier which I had cooling on a rack on the counter. Contrary to my ban on animal products, I had given in to eating eggs and milk in the pie. I figured I'd feel bad about my lapse in vegetarian ethics after I ate. Faust had made a point of repeatedly sniffing the dessert.

Though I never saw his tongue actually scrape across the custard's surface, I wasn't optimistic he wouldn't be sharing his saliva with me. After we dined together as usual, I gave him his own small slice of pie. Despite the allspice, cloves, nutmeg, cinnamon, and mace I had liberally mixed in the filling, he ate it with relish, inelegantly smacking his kitty lips. As I ate, I closed my eyes. If tongue tracks existed on my piece, I did not want to see them.

CHAPTER 16

MEETING WINTER HEAD ON
✳✳

When the first snowfall blanketed the yard and heavily laden the tree branches, Faust could not wait to go outside. Bicycling was now totally out of the question so I dressed him in his harness, swept the back steps with an old straw broom, and led him into the glaringly-white back yard. There he promptly disappeared beneath the snow. Up popped a gray and white head, amber eyes wide open, and mite-free ears erect. He was obviously surprised he could not walk on top of this white mattress cover-like surface.

Then like a fox in search of a rodent, he jumped up and disappeared again head first, tunneling toward the dogwood tree, using his nose as a snowplow. Maybe he didn't really want to walk on top of it after all. Up he came again, whiskers and eyebrows covered with snow crystals. This time, he acted like a snow blower, charging with his head slightly raised, throwing snow into the air on both sides of the deep path he was creating.

What Faust the Dancing Cat Taught Me

In the past as a homeless cat he surely had to protect himself from this cold precipitation but now he could take full advantage of it with his healthy, fully-fleshed body, and warm accommodations to retire to. He was doing just that. No holds barred. He was enjoying himself with wild abandon. Above my shins in snow without boots, I followed him around until he began to tire. I scooped him up to go back inside. This was not what he wanted and he made his displeasure loudly known. Scratching the back door, he turned and looked at me, making sure he had my attention, and mouhwed mournfully.

At this, I plopped him on my lap, removed his wet harness, and with a hand towel rubbed him dry. This is despite the fact he really wasn't wet. His guard hairs had protected him from the moisture. As he looked at me pitifully, I promised I would take him out again later. Having gotten what he wanted, at least in part, he then raised an eyebrow as if letting me know he was not pleased he had to wait. Wasn't there something he could do to convince me that sooner was better than later? When that didn't work, he ran back to the door, to show me he would hold me to that as a sacred promise. I've found that you should never promise anything to a cat you won't follow through on. They are really big on trust and respect ... that's both giving and receiving. I'm convinced they keep an accounting, a running tally, in their heads about what you say you'll do and what you actually do.

Since I was being so ingratiating, he apparently thought he might make the most of it. No longer scratching the back door, he went into the kitchen, leapt onto the counter, pawed open the upper cabinet door behind which his treats were stored. He stood up, grabbed the bag in his teeth, and jumped down with it. When he brought it to me, I suddenly felt like Dr. Frankenstein. I had created a monster that I no longer had control over. I was at its mercy.

After munching a few obligatory treats, he climbed up his cat tree to watch as the birds used their feet to brush away snow from their wooden feeder perches outside his window. He didn't bother chattering at them. He knew they would only have mocked his behavior, saying, "Nyaggh, nyaggh, you can't get to us!"

As I sat with the bag of treat in my hand, I thought the least he could have done was to return the bag to the cabinet where he had gotten it. But then again I was his servant and should know by now such things were not going to happen. Besides, cats don't necessarily meet human expectations—whether those expectations are realistic or not. If asked, cats will no doubt tell you: We were not put here on earth for you or to do you bidding. Deal with it.

CHAPTER 17

SINGING 'TIS THE SEASON

✷✷

As Christmas was close at hand, I decided against a large cut tree. I was thinking more along the lines of a smaller living tree I could give to a friend as a gift after the holiday to add to their landscaping. Until I had my own house, I wouldn't be planting any conifers. At a nursery in Wayland, Faust and I found the perfect four-footer. With the height of its pot it was six feet.

In my enthusiasm I had not considered not only the weight of this tree but also how I'd transport it in my Rabbit. A young man, who was fascinated by Faust lounging around my shoulders, hoisted the noble fir onto a dolly for me then rolled it to my car. I put down the back seat, leaving a near flat surface. I had a large blue plastic tarp I spread out. The young man, grunting, lifted it on to the tailgate.

With the tree nearly horizontal, he rolled and pushed and pulled and rolled it until the tree occupied the rear of the car on a diagonal. But I couldn't travel back to

Sudbury with the tailgate open. Also I didn't have anything with which to secure the hatch to the tailgate so the back window wouldn't be flapping in the breeze. I knew the tree was unlikely to fall out. But it would have been just my luck for a cop to fine me for not having had a red flag attached to the projection. So, even with my potentially damaging the tree top, I crossed my fingers and hoped for the best. I slowly raised the tailgate and lowered the hatchback door to lock the assembly.

Getting this tree in the house was the really big problem. I unattached Faust, locked him in the bathroom off the kitchen, and started working on jockeying the tree out of the car. I had no idea what it weighed—maybe eighty pounds, maybe sixty. All I knew was it was a heavy sucker and exceedingly awkward to handle. It slid off the tailgate with a crash, cracking its large black plastic pot. Great, I thought, and found some duct tape to wrap around the pot to keep it from peppering the house with its black soil. I rolled it on its bottom edge this way then that in the garage until I reached the concrete step into the house.

Bending my knees, I took a deep breath, and tried to lift it, exhaling as I did. Only the rim of the black pot was on the step, the tree leaning back against me. I shimmied forward to get more of the pot flat on the step. I was sweating and panting, now unhappy with myself for not having taken up weight lifting. The fire door from the kitchen to the garage kept closing, bumping into me. But with another lift and several more grunts. I made it into the kitchen where I wriggled it onto a throw rug. From there I dragged it, careful of my back and sciatic nerve, into the living room. I released Faust who likewise marveled at our newest live acquisition.

It was beautiful. I'd put a pan under the pot to catch the water from watering the tree then drape the pot with some red furry acrylic fabric I had from which I had made stockings to hang from the mantelpiece. I had some old hand-blown Norwegian glass ornaments my mother had brought with her from her birthplace in Trondheim. There were bells, balls, stars, graceful birds with long Fiberglas tails, musical instruments, and Santa heads. There were also fancy multi-colored delicate glass chains. I went to the downstairs closet for that box of Christmas decorations. Faust followed me sure I was up to something intriguing. As I sat on the living room floor, I pulled out a string of smaller lights, thinking the small tree would be dwarfed by regular-size bulbs. Faust watched with interest.

Slowly, layer by layer, the tree was taking shape, looking as festive as I hoped it would be. Before I put cotton on the branches to simulate snow and the silver

Mylar strips like rain, I carefully added all the glass ornaments the tree could safely and aesthetically hold. I plugged in the lights and enjoyed the warmth of the holiday vision. Faust curled up in my lap on the floor, enrapt, gazing at the lights as well. The rest of the evening we had dinner and watched Nature about wild horses and a Nova about pollution of the Hudson River on PBS.

Crash. The red numbers indicating 3:04 a.m. glared at me in the dark. I'd heard something that startled me from a sound sleep. I couldn't tell if an intruder had tried to break in or something had fallen. With my moccasins on, I turned on all the lights. Might as well let the prowler know I was up and give it time to get away. A Louisville Slugger baseball bat in hand from the closet, I made my way carefully down the hall.

There in the living room I saw it. It was what I had suspected from the moment I'd heard the crash. Faust was stuck in the branches of the fir, struggling to extricate himself. In doing so he had knocked several glass ornaments off, smashing them on the floor. My still-asleep brain said, Now what? What do I do first? Extricate Faust? Or clean up the broken glass slivers?

Yawning, I reached around him to remove any ornaments nearby his caught limbs. After I placed them on the floor, I disentangled him. He had small droplets of sap on his fur but no glass shards on him or on his paws. After locking him again in the bathroom, I cleaned up the dangerous mess. Then using small amounts of turpentine which I followed with shampoo, I carefully removed the viscous sap dotting his coat.

I shook my head, wondering why I hadn't considered this before buying and decorating the tree. I felt so stupid. As much as Faust and I were close companions, he was still a cat and did was cats naturally do. They explore and they climb. I sighed and pulled out the box again to replace the remaining ornaments, rain, cotton, and lights. There was no question. Faust was going to try this again. How could he resist the challenge. If I were a cat, I wouldn't. I'd have to figure out something else.

But at that moment I needed sleep more than a new Christmas tree. Faust jumped onto the bed and snuggled around my head on the pillow, like a shapka, a Russian fur hat. As I lay in bed, the thought about hanging a small fake tree from the ceiling occurred to me, but I dismissed it. I could drape Faust's kitty tree with ornaments but those decorations too would be destroyed as easily as those on the living tree. I hoped in a couple of hours my brain synapses would produce a solution while I slept.

As I had my granola and hot black cherry tea, I scanned the living room for ideas. The mantelpiece was out. He could jump onto it. There was a plain chandelier in the dining room but Faust could levitate to it also if he were sufficiently curious. Then my eye stopped on my split-leaf philodendron (aka *monstera deliciosa*). I had had this from a small plant and had babied it into this six-foot tower of green. Native to tropical rainforests, it has large, leathery, glossy heart-shaped leaves with holes, producing lobed leaves. It likes high humidity and shade. Faust had never bothered it. Perhaps that was because of the downward hanging leaves and very flexible leaf stalks.

Why not? I thought. I couldn't put lights on it because they might burn the leaves, but I could put just about anything else I wanted on it to decorate it. But using a lot of the paper decorations my mother and I had made when I was in sixth grade would be better than anything glass ... in case. I had kept them as a tribute to her artistic innovation.

After working on two of my projects—one was writing creative job hunting white paper and other was editing the results of a behavioral experiment on truth telling, I found the old box of the less fragile ornaments. I set to work with Faust at my side, practicing his sitting up waving. Where had he learned that? From the raccoon he had seen on Nature?

Despite my unusual Christmas "tree," it looked particularly festive when we were all finished. I say "we" because Faust helped by carrying the colored paper chains along the floor from room to room, ostensibly to "unknot" them for me. All the balls were very light-weight, having been made from *papier mâché* and covered in still-sparkling glitter. There were woven German stars, Santa mobiles, and myriad pipe-cleaner people wrapped in wool singing with music books and skiing with poles and skis. I topped the plant with a gold foil porcupine Polish star.

Maybe, I thought, I should get some cranberries to string as well. That would add a further red draping effect. Furthermore, if Faust happened to capture and eat one, it wouldn't be poisonous to him, unlike raisins. Finally I wrapped the philodendron's pot in the furry red acrylic fabric I was going to use on my living tree. Now I had only to make and stuff a stocking for Faust to hang from the mantelpiece and await Christmas Day.

Christmas Day arrived early. I was awakened around 6 a.m. to the sound of ripping and tearing paper. That was something I had always wanted to do as a child but was too afraid to risk being punished for the" unacceptable" behavior.

What Faust the Dancing Cat Taught Me

Faust had checked out all the gifts under the tree and located some catnip toys. He knew they would "turn bad," "melt," or "mold" if he didn't open them right away.

Putting on the kettle to boil for tea, I wrapped my robe around me, put on some orchestral Christmas music, and settled on the floor. Faust had already gummed the tail off a super-saturated catnip mouse. Glassy-eyed, he began plowing through everything under the tree, turning on a dime, and retracing his steps as packages fell hither and thither. Then he hopped on my lap, crawled up my front, licked my face, and jumped down to resume his rampage.

When he came down from his amphetamine-like high, I helped him open his other gifts. He received a ten-inch-diameter, blue, hollow, doughnut-shaped toy that had a ball in its inner ring. If he pushed the ball with his paw, it would roll around the doughnut and he could chase it. He tried it once then went back to the Christmas wrappings. He received a wand that had a long string at the end to which was attached a silvery-Mylar pompom. He swatted it a couple of times then went back to the paper. He received a hard rubber ball with a jingle bell inside. He batted it once.

Then he found what he had really wanted above all else. It was the smallish box the doughnut toy came in. He stripped the wrapping paper from its exterior and squeezed his body into it. His rump and tail hung out and his head was buried in his abdomen. It was there he fell asleep with a silly smile on his face.

For the party for friends from Nahant, Framingham, and Wellesley to exchange gifts and celebrate, I had made a variety of yummy canapés. We had boiled shrimp, smoked salmon, Norwegian *gjetost* (goat cheese), Brie, raw vegetables with a tofu-pesto-spinach-garlic dip, all kinds of crackers and chips, hot salsa, and guacamole.

Faust sat primly on his cat tree, away from the dining room table on which the feast was displayed. He looked alert, ears erect, trying to catch the attention of any and all guests who felt obligated to fawn all over him. Being on his best behavior, he was on the receiving end of gifts of shrimp, salmon, and goat cheese which his followers slipped to him as unobtrusively as possible so I wouldn't know. Right. Again he was king overlooking his domain, directing his subjects with a velvet-gloved gauntlet.

Later after everyone had left, Faust and I would have Christmas dinner. I wasn't sure how interested he would be after all the rich food he had "secretly" devoured that afternoon. I presented him with Friskies turkey paté, a tiny bit of cranberry sauce, some salad greens, and an itty-bitty slice of pumpkin pie. He even had a lick of the nonalcoholic eggnog left over from the afternoon's party—I had had bourbon and rum available for anyone who wanted a little kick to their holiday cup of cheer.

Following dinner, we watched the inimitable Alistair Sim in "Scrooge," the 1951 version of "A Christmas Carol." After Ebenezer has been visited by the three spirits (Christmas Past, Christmas Present, and Christmas Future), he discovers he could change his life and future for the better. What likely lay ahead of him otherwise is more than a little grim and unnerving. Having awakened to find he hadn't missed Christmas Day, he begins whooping and hollering all around his bedroom. I considered it was one of the funniest, all-time manically-eccentric, and wonderful performances of Sim's long film career.

Faust, who was drifting off on the sofa beside me, awoke with a start. He looked at Sim and cocked his head. Suddenly he slipped off the cushion and joined in the dancing. In front of the television to my utter amazement, he waltzed, circled, and dipped. He raised his paw in a wave at me, then rolled over from side to side. He followed that with a somersault and the back flip he had executed on the beach at Rockport. I thought, This can't possibly be. I must be hallucinating, or at the very least, imagining this. He ended his performance with a walk from the television to me on his hind legs. There upon, he tapped my foot and leapt onto my shoulders with a big slurp on my face.

Of all the gifts I had received that day, or would ever receive, that was by far the most wonderful, loving, and caring gift he, or anyone, could possibly have given me ... then ... or at any time. "Thank you, my sweet, talented Faust."

CHAPTER 18

DRIVING TO FLORIDA
✹✹

It was quite a number of years after my mother's divorce from my emotionally impaired father that she decided she wanted to move to New Port Richey, Florida. She had had enough of shoveling snow, chipping ice off her windshield, and driving on slippery streets. She had picked New Port Richey, near the sponge-capital of the U.S., Tarpon Springs, because several of her sales colleagues from the exclusive dress shop where she had worked in Framingham Shoppers' World had moved there. They were enjoying the sunshine and tropical warmth and worked on her to lure her to come their way.

Since I was going to help her move and didn't know how long I'd be gone, I was not about to leave Faust behind with a pet sitter, even one with stellar credentials and testimonials from the American Society for the Prevention of Cruelty to Animals. So after packing the small U-Haul trailer and Mother's station wagon, I added my suitcase, Faust's essentials, and Faust.

Ready to leave early one snowy morning, we had planned to use Interstate-95 all the way south. The first leg of the trip, Boston to Washington, D.C., was about eight hours, at least in ideal driving conditions, which we did not have. We wanted to drive no more than ten hours a day depending upon the weather. If we ran into a heavy snow storm, it would have to be much shorter and we would take our chances finding a place to stay. Likely as not, Virginia would be our first stop for the night, unless... .

While we took turns driving, I mostly navigated using an AAA Triptik, likewise directing Faust's gaze to points of interest. The biggest point of interest for a while was the pig-hauling truck we were stuck behind going five miles per hour on the New Jersey Turnpike. A several-car accident had occurred up ahead resulting from one car spinning out of control on an icy patch with others doing the same as they tried to pass the first car, creating this traffic jam. Even with our windows closed we were gagging from the smell. The car heater only seemed to exacerbate it so we turned it off. But our feet were soon too cold to keep the heater off for long.

Even in the cold, the smell permeated the car. I hated to imagine how grotesque it must have smelled on a hot, humid day. Was that just from the pigs immediately being transported? Or were those trucks never cleaned? I wondered. Would sufficient straw catch and help deodorize the excrement? Poor pigs. Poor us.

While I was desperately searching for a handkerchief to cover my nose and mouth, I wished for a miracle to occur, to have some Vicks VapoRub materialize to smear on my upper lip. Faust was pacing on the dashboard, trying to see what was in the truck. The smell seemed to intrigue rather than offend him. We tried our best to suffer in silence but when you think you may just start to puke and never stop, it is hard to keep from grunting, groaning, and clearing your throat.

Twenty minutes later we were free to continue our trip. As we drove past the pig truck, Faust stared. He actually looked as if he felt sorry for their cramped, filthy transport conditions as well as for the pigs' likely destination. It was as if he were thinking that while pigs were inferior to cats, they were still intelligent and should be treated with respect. Moreover, they should not be slaughtered. Even though Faust considered dogs to be low man on the sentient-beings' values totem pole, he felt they should not be torturously slaughtered, skinned for their fur, eaten as they were in some countries, or penned in small enclosures to mass-produce puppies.

Faust seemed deeply enmeshed in philosophic thought after we had left the pig truck in our wake. I had never seen him like this before. It was if he were weighing the ends of providing food against the means of producers treating sentient beings any way they wanted, even abusing them in the process. As he sat in thought, we opened the windows for a few minutes, despite the cold, to replace the air. I couldn't imagine anything more obnoxious and nauseating than the smell of pig excrement.

That night, exhausted from the slushy, snowy, icy road conditions, we arrived at a Best Western motel on the south side of Richmond, Virginia, an area surrounded by numerous battlefields which we did not have time to visit. I left Faust in our room as we looked for food to bring back. Their restaurant had some overcooked fish he and I could share, a small salad consisting mostly of iceberg lettuce and a few wrinkled tomato wedges, milk for him and tea for me. My mother ordered a medium-rare steak with mashed potatoes smothered in sour cream and chives, green beans with deep-fried onion rings, and coffee.

Faust looked expectant as we unwrapped what he was sure was his own kitty buffet. On his own chair, I gave him a bread and butter plate with some pan-fried trout, a tiny piece of steak, a gift from my mother, and some salad greens. I had gotten a glass of milk for him, hoping that just a little wouldn't give him diarrhea while on the road. He ate daintily but felt compelled to check all the goodies that decorated my mother's copiously-filled plate. He didn't need to do mine. He knew it was same old, same old.

As he did that, my anxiety rose. I was sure my mother was going to start screaming at him for sniffing and touching her dish. She had always been hyper-tense when I was younger about animals at the table. Whispering, "Faust," I tried to redirect him but he would have none of it. Just as my mother raised her steak-speared fork to her mouth, Faust touched the fork, angling it toward him, releasing the piece of meat from the fork tines with his paw, and gobbling it up. I died a thousand torturous deaths because she was going to start shouting at the top of her lungs, angry about his uncivil behavior. I quickly grabbed him, put him on the floor, and began my most heart-rending apology. "I'm so sorry. He knows better than that. If he licked your food—I don't think he did—but if he did, I'll get you a replacement. I'll make sure he doesn't do it again."

"Did you teach him to do that?" she asked.

"Huh? No, no! I had no idea he would touch your food." I was groveling, begging for absolution. "I'm so sorry. I'll watch him more carefully when we eat."

"You know that took a lot of calculation and deft movement to do that." She turned to Faust and said further, "If you want another piece, just ask me and I'll give you some."

What? What had she just said? Who was this person? This was not my mother. This must have been my "anti-matter" mother. I was definitely in another, parallel universe or in the Twilight Zone. My real mother would have laid down the law, segueing into what etiquette demands even of animals, and how animals have NO place at the table because it was disgusting if they touched your food. You had no idea where their paws, not to mention their tongues, had been. (Well, not exactly. I knew precisely where his paws and tongue had been and I wasn't eager for either of them to touch anything that entered my mouth.)

I was taken aback. Smiling, she looked at me and said, "You have a very nice, well-behaved cat." Was she being sarcastic? She had a history of being sarcastic, even nasty. I nodded a thank you just in case she wasn't, but was still looking at her questioningly. I never figured that one out and wasn't about to ask.

The next morning before starting the next leg of our trip, we wanted to look for some interesting carved wood pieces, especially animals done by artisans from the Cherokee Nation. After locating a long parking space for the car and trailer, we wrapped our coats around us, with Faust acting as my muffler, and visited a few of the galleries. Mother found an owl carved from the highly-prized mountain laurel root burl she liked and I purchased what looked like both a fox and a coyote done in butternut, which is like white walnut. Whichever it was didn't matter because it was beautifully done, with long lean lines.

As we were still looking around, Faust spotted a small, black and white dog, with a short tail, erect ears, and slightly bulging eyes—a Boston Terrier to be precise. Because of its pushed in nose which inhibited its breathing, it was constantly snorting and snuffling. It had just entered the shop by itself, apparently without a human companion.

The dog spotted me and began its piercing yipping which screeched at me like fingernails on a blackboard. The next thing I knew it had raced up to me, seized my leg with its paws like wrestler with a hammerlock. Then it began humping as if inspired by a Viagra commercial.

"Go away!" I spoke harshly to it, as I shook my leg. Faust stayed in place using his claws, as I hopped on one foot. The dog hung on like a shark on a seal, now moving its lower body with even more sexual fervor.

Faust growled. "I said 'get away,' you disgusting creature! Go find yourself a female dog, if she'll have you." Bracing Faust with one hand, I leaned over and with my free hand shoved the canine pervert off to the side. It slid two feet across the floor, stopping short of the wall.

The proprietor who was wrapping our purchases in back apparently had not witnessed this or was laughing too hard to show himself just yet. The dog, however, was not through with me. He sat there for a moment as if trying to regain some of his dignity. Faust would have mightily disagreed with this assessment because he knew for a fact dogs had no real dignity to regain. After all, if they would allow themselves to have "masters" (cats did *not* have "masters") ... . Faust did not get the chance to finish his discriminatory thought.

The dog apparently had decided it was not about to take my behavior lying down ... and had constructed a plan. Stealthily it crept up behind me. Stopping its snuffling just long enough so I wouldn't hear it, it lifted his leg, letting loose the Johnstown flood, soaking my pant leg, athletic sock, and New Balance running shoe. "You little son of a bitch!" I shouted at it. If dogs could snicker, it did, sitting there immensely enjoying my urine-soaked anger and its revenge.

Just then the proprietor returned, saw the Charles Manson-crazed expression on my downturned face and the puddle on his wood floor. "I'm so sorry. That's the dog from next door." That was it. I was considering tying the dog to two opposing horses and cracking a whip. Faust had turned his body around over my right shoulder, arching his back like a Halloween cat and hissing, to glare at the offending canine as it perpetrated its act. He seemed to be debating whether to climb down and give the dog a piece of his mind and a few well-placed claws and teeth.

He was in the mood to scare the shit out of him and actually would have relished the interaction. How dare that lowest-of-the-low being whiz on my human? There were rules of etiquette and certainly the Geneva Conventions about conduct of war by which to abide. I scratched Faust under the chin and whispered, "Don't bother. He probably has fleas ... and, heaven forbid, might snort or fart on you." Faust gave the dog his best "you scum of the earth" look.

I drew in a lung-filling breath. Like a diplomat on the verge of an argument with a recalcitrant national figure about their unsupportable foreign policy, I put my hand up to stop further explanations from the proprietor. Then the dog ran out the front door as fast as its stubby legs could carry it. I gathered all my own dignity, serenity, and our purchases from the proprietor's hands, nodded a farewell, and left, with one foot sloshing.

Now I had to go back to the car to change from my pee-dyed pants, sock, and shoe. I spoke to my mother, who couldn't respond. She was leaning on the car, doubled-over, holding her stomach, laughing. "Yeah, the dog was a real card," I said. "However, I have to find a place where I can wash, or at least rinse, these before we go. I don't want to travel with dog urine in the back of the car adding to the indoor ambiance." My mother, still doubled over, waved at me to let me know she had heard me but still couldn't respond.

With items from my suitcase, I stepped inside the trailer with just barely room enough to turn around if I stood on her plastic-covered sofa, dripping, to change. I placed my marinaded apparel in a grocery bag to look for a Laundromat. It was a good thing I had at the last minute decided to bring an extra pair of shoes which I didn't think I'd need. Asking around, we found a Laundromat down a side street, several blocks away from the galleries.

While at the Laundromat, Faust sat directly in front of the front-loading washing machine and followed the motion with his head. He seemed fascinated by it. I was waiting for him to start to fall over from dizziness, which he didn't. Instead, he simply re-cocked his head to the other side and focused on the running shoe when it appeared. It was twisting and turning, wet laces flying, and thumping loudly as it hit the rotating cylinder.

When the clothes moved to the dryer, he suddenly jumped onto the vibrating machine, circled twice and settled in. Whatever was still not dry after one go 'round, specifically my running shoe, I would hang in the back of the car to dry. Hopefully the sun and the heater-generated moving air would help over the remainder of our trip. My mother finally finished her laughing fit with only a couple of snorts. I was still pissed off. Damn dog!

CHAPTER 19

ENCOUNTERING A REDNECK COP

✸✸

We arrived late at the Best Western in New Port Richey and temporarily unpacked. Early the next morning we met with a realtor Mother had contacted by phone before we left Massachusetts. Consequently she already had several apartments to show her. Faust was quite adamant about not staying in some strange motel room by himself. To the discomfort of the realtor who perhaps feared cat hair or scratches on her upholstery even though she didn't say anything aloud, he wrapped himself around my neck and stayed there. He was on his best behavior as she escorted us around.

The first apartment in a three-story white-stucco-ed building was several flights up and overlooked a basketball court where six noisy children were repeatedly bouncing the ball, trying to imitate the techniques of the Harlem Globetrotters. The second apartment was pink stuccoed one-floor with shady trees in small grassy patches at both the front and sliding-glass back door. It was a sunny, two-bedroom with cross ventilation and the bonus of squirrels and ducks that visited. Mother snatched it up.

Over the next two days, we moved her in, with Faust locked in the bathroom to keep him from getting underfoot or making friends with the squirrels or ducks. Besides I wasn't crazy about the idea of him running on the grassy patch by the back door where the ducks frequently defecated. Relegated to this white-tiled prison, he complained bitterly. Leaping against the door and jiggling the door knob, he mouhwed every time someone passed. Having the safety key to open a locked door from the outside, I had locked Faust's door. I kept waiting for Mother to complain about the "infernal racket," but she never did. Things had changed for the better for her since her divorce from my father. I was pleased for her.

The next morning after dropping off the U-Haul trailer, mother set out to drive me and Faust to the Tampa Airport to catch our flight back to Boston. Sunny and warm, it was commuter time with bumper-to-bumper traffic. Traveling the posted speed limit, we stayed in the left lane because the turn for the airport was coming up but we weren't sure exactly where. We had been unable to get specific directions before we left—"approximately ten miles up the highway."

The next thing we knew a police car pulled in behind us with its flashers and siren on. The driver motioned for us to move to the right lane and then off on the side of the road. What could we have done? With perhaps a sense of foreboding, Faust disappeared under the front seat. The cop waited a few minutes before alighting from his car. I wondered if he were checking on our Massachusetts license plate ... or just trying to make us sweat a little.

The heavy-set officer in a beige uniform that clung to his beer belly swaggered over to us. Mother rolled down her window, "Yes, officer, what's the problem?"

He snickered. "I see you two ladies are from Mass-a-TOO-setts." This was not starting well. "Don't they teach you how to drive in Mass-a-TOO-setts?" he asked condescendingly.

Mother obviously restraining herself, said, "I don't understand. We were doing the speed limit."

"Well," he puffed out his chest and snickered again, "you were driving too slow for the left lane."

"We were in the left lane because we are going to the airport. We were in the right lane in this heavy traffic and moved over when we had the chance. We were concerned if we stayed in the right lane, we wouldn't be able to get over in time to make our left turn."

"That's no excuse." All but shaking his finger at us, he leaned into the driver's side window close to Mother's face, significantly invading her personal space. He said accusingly, "You have been creating a traffic jam for miles and miles and miles by going so slowly."

Having kept an eye on traffic all around us, I did not believe that statement for one minute. We were right behind the car in front. He was all about intimidating us and enjoying himself in the process. My mother continued, "Are you saying, officer, that we should have been ignoring the speed limit?"

Frowning, he was not sure how to interpret what sounded to him possibly like sarcasm. Could this woman be using sarcasm with me? Could she be that smart ... or that reckless? While he had been reveling in his fun with the female out-of-staters, it was now getting tedious for him. It appeared he was particularly annoyed we weren't getting all upset that he might give us a ticket. Moreover, we weren't flirting with him, using our so-called "feminine wiles," or getting down on bended knee to beg for his forgiveness for our transgressions. I suspect he expected and desired at least one of those behaviors.

"I could give you little ladies from Mass-a-TOO-setts a ticket. But," he added a long pregnant pause, "I won't ... this time." I thought, Yeah, big deal. "Still, ignorance of the law is no excuse, neither is lack of common sense, even for you Yankee ladies." He laughed at his clever retort which made his jowls sway.

As he strode away, my mother called after him with incredible pleasantness, "Officer, so we won't repeat our error (I nearly choked on her underlying, not so subtle, snide intention), where is the left turn for the airport?"

As if having to respond to those "damned Yankees" and females at that was above and beyond the call of duty, for which he truly deserved hazardous duty pay, he called over his shoulder, "Two miles ahead."

We rolled our eyes, shook our heads, and started giggling. It was only partly as a release from the tension of the encounter. "Little ladies? Yankees? Mass-a-TOO-setts? *Our* ignorance? Our lack of common sense? Can you believe what just happened? This is a fine howdy-doo and Welcome to Florida! Ooh, I think we just met our first honest-to-goodness redneck Southern cop. Lordy! What a misogynist! It's been a real pleasure! Let's do it again some time."

Faust re-appeared, eyes narrowed. Being very protective, he didn't like the cop's attitude or behavior. After a few moments, he cautiously peered over the dashboard through the windshield. He saw the cop get into his car, make the traffic part like the Red Sea for him, and drive off ... in the left lane.

Making a sneezing sound in the cruiser's direction, Faust rubbed his right paw against his nostrils—which I thought was a very fine simulation of his thumbing his nose. Then he settled himself on my lap again. However, his upturned upper lip, looking as if he were smelling cabbage, suggested he was still unhappy that this un-cat-like bozo had talked to his humans that way. The incredible nerve of him. This "lowest of dogs" would surely get his comeuppance someday ... and he hoped a cat would be there to witness it ... if not initiate it.

CHAPTER 20

TAKING TO THE AIR

✳✳

For our flight I had gotten one of those required, perfunctory tiny under-the-seat airline carriers for Faust. I couldn't imagine how any animal, except perhaps a small mouse, could do anything but hunker down in it. Fortunately many years later they finally allowed decent-sized carriers. The seats beside me were empty. Once the Delta flight was airborne, I carefully lifted Faust's plastic isolation cell onto my lap. He looked at me sadly through the openings, barely able to raise his head, and begged to be released. I undid the latch and let the top drop. He stretched his body as if doing the Cobra yoga position then rubbed his head against my arm as a thank you.

I whispered to him, "If I put the open carrier on the seat next to me, will you stay in it?" He lifted his whiskers, making sure I saw his elongated eye teeth of which he was so proud. Of course, that didn't mean he would stay in it. He didn't. So much for our reaching an agreement. He immediately crawled onto my lap, purring.

The air was getting smoky since smoking had not yet been prohibited in planes and the smoke easily traveled over the non-existent No-Smoking Section boundary. Being allergic to tobacco smoke, I was getting a headache, stuffy nose, and a sore throat and I worried about Faust's less than fully-functioning lungs breathing in all that carcinogenic particulate matter and carbon monoxide. The flight attendant walked by, then stopped when she saw the curled up ball of gray and white fluff. "You know you're supposed to keep animals under your seat."

I replied, "I know but he could barely breathe much less move or sleep in that small contraption. Can you imagine having to tolerate that for hours? It's like a straitjacket."

"Well, no, I can't imagine it," she confided. "Don't tell anyone I told you this but I think it looks like some kind of torture box. I let a little dog out too." She turned around and pointed forward. "Just don't let him get loose." She gave Faust a friendly pat on the head to which he immediately reciprocated with a cheek rub on her hand. That changed her tone from official to human. "What its name?" she asked.

"Faust."

"No kidding. Great name. Does he fly often?"

"He travels a good deal but this is his very first flight and you're now making it very pleasant for him. Thank you. I'm sure he appreciates it."

She smiled broadly. "Can I get him anything? I might have some milk in the galley."

"Not just yet, thanks for asking. He's had a busy morning."

"I'll be by in a little while to check on him." She smiled again ... not at me, at Faust. When he's around, I sometimes feel like chopped liver.

She went off to start serving coffee. Faust looked at me, lifted his whiskers, and stood up to look out the porthole. Suddenly there was a terrible inhuman scream. It sounded like what I imagined if someone had been attacked by a lion that had torn off their arm ... or they had swallowed their dentures. "Oh! Owwww! No!" Followed by a gasping, strangled, "Oh my God! It's a cat! Stewardess, help, help! That is NOT allowed in here! Stewardness, get rid of it!"

I looked around to see where it was coming from. It was emanating from a heavily made up, hair-sprayed, bejeweled, adipose older woman wearing a tight purple dress two rows in front of us on the other side. She was holding a small, un-caged silver and beige fluff ball with jet-black button eyes—a Yorkshire Terrier. It was probably the one to which the attendant had referred. It sported a red bow on its forelock and crimson toenails. She was looking straight at me, sputtering, waving her arms, repeatedly stabbing the flight attendant's buzzer.

Our attendant arrived to address the commotion. "Madam, what is the problem? How may I help you?"

"There's ... there's ... oh, my God! There's a CAT over there," she rasped, pointing at Faust who was still standing motionless on my lap, engrossed in the rough sea of clouds over which we were flying

"Yes, he is being let out of his restrictive carrier for a little bit ... just like your little dog."

"But, cats should not be allowed out of their carriers. Cats should not be allowed to fly with humans. They're dirty. They're full of pests and diseases. They kill songbirds. They dig up rose gardens. They attack little dogs. They scratch and bite. They're a danger to pregnant women." She hugged her little dog who barely responded. "They should be kept with the luggage and freight below. It's not safe. It's just not right. They're evil, disgusting animals! I don't want my 'Precious Jewel,'" nodding at her tiny dog, "anywhere near them. That's why I always fly first-class but ... I couldn't get a seat at the last minute so ... regretfully ... I'm back here, being subjected to ... a cat!"

"Cats, like dogs, are allowed in all sections of the cabin. But I can see you're upset. May I get you a drink and a snack on Delta? Would your dog like anything? If the cat moves, I'll have it put back in its carrier immediately. Is that okay?"

"But ... but ... You're sure you can't get rid of it? Don't you have a way of putting it in the overhead storage if you can't put in the hold?" The attendant kept her smile in place, apparently not seeing any benefit in mentioning the cat's suffocation in the storage bin which the woman might have enjoyed considering. She waited.

"A drink?" the woman finally responded seeing she wasn't going to get her way with respect to the cat. "Well, ... I guess so. Then make that a double vodka and tonic and whatever you have to eat. I'm sure my sugar is low after this terrible shock."

She began fanning herself dramatically with her hand. It was as if because of the "horror" she had just witnessed she might succumb to the vapors. "And you'll be sure to have *it* put back in *its* box if *it* moves?" The attendant nodded and smiled reassuringly. As she made her way back down the aisle to get the double vodka and tonic, she reached over to stroke Faust's back and winked at me. Faust lifted his whiskers, revealed his fangs, then rubbed her hand again and gave her a lick. Letting out a giggle at the sight of his Halloweenprank teeth, she smiled broadly and gratefully and continued her journey to the galley.

Occasionally the distraught woman two rows up would crane her neck to check on Faust. But she could see nothing to further support her complaints of Faust "contaminating" her pooch or her. That she could say nothing further seemed to distress her even more, leaving her fidgeting in her seat with her quiet, apparently sedated, toy animal ensconced on her lap. By the time we reached Logan Airport in Boston, however, she was dozing noisily. Hopefully she was dreaming about being covered in fleas and tapeworms, on her knees, obeying the every whim of a cat in a dominatrix's black leather outfit, looming over her with whip in hand.

It was a little over a year that Faust had come into and graced my life. Since his first attempts at opening closed doors, he had become an expert. No closed door in the house held him at bay unless it was locked and did not have a key in the lock. Having perfected his technique, he no longer made the battering noise he had initially. Now he silently jumped up at the door knob, clasped it with both front paws and swung his body from side to side. In only a second or two, the door swung slowly open. He then jumped down, bumped it with his head if absolutely necessary, and casually entered.

It was obvious to me that in "his house" he felt no room should be off-limits. No nook or cranny should be unavailable to him. His sense of privacy was really no different from mine. He wanted privacy when he used his litter pan. He would use it when I was in the bathroom with him but he would have preferred to have a three-panel screen in front of it at those times. He wanted privacy when he didn't feel well. Like other cats, he didn't want to share his pain, discomfort, or illness. Furthermore, he wanted privacy if he happened to catch a mouse. If he had excelled at a demonstration of his predatory skills, he surely didn't want some human blundering into his private celebration, ruining everything. Besides, humans were likely not to understand what the mouse trophy really meant and try to remove it or, if still alive, set it free outside.

But other than that, everything was his to access and rule. I would have to keep this in mind for whenever we traveled. And likewise keep it in mind when we had guests. I would suggest they lock their doors because in this establishment, cats rule. Besides, there is nothing quite so disconcerting as waking up in the morning with a cat standing on your chest, staring you in the face.

CHAPTER 21

PLAYING THE HAMMERED DULCIMER

✳✳

After I had discovered the musical instrument that played the "Gaspé Reel" on Crockett's Victory Garden, I learned about Andy's Front Hall in Voorheesville, New York. Andy and Bill Spence, of the Fennig All-Stars' fame, had a mail-order music business, which had records, cassette tapes, instructions for building hammered dulcimers, books of music, and musical instruments of all kinds.

The idea of working with wood and creating my own musical instrument intrigued me. But given the physics involved in creating the soundboard, placing the bridges just right on it, adding tuning pins and the strings, and tightening them appropriately, I decided against it. There were too many things I could mess up. Then what would I do? Call Bill Spence and travel to Voorheesville to have him fix it for a hefty price? That wasn't an inviting thought.

Perhaps I should purchase one already made. But that too was problematic. How would I know how that particular instrument sounded ahead of time? Rather than purchase just anything from a catalogue, I continued to look for a seller where I could hear and try the instrument or a maker whose artistry I likewise could sample. That slowed me down.

In the interim I was building a nice record collection of albums by hammered dulcimer artists, both old and new. I had albums by the progenitors of today's hammered dulcimer music, like Chet Parker and Paul Van Arsdale. I had up-and-comers, like John McCutcheon, Guy Carawan, Walt Michael, and, of course, Bill Spence. Front Hall mailed a pulp-paper catalogue every couple of months which also had announcements of folk music events. One that caught my eye was The Cranberry Dulcimer Gathering in Binghamton, New York.

"Faust," I called with some excitement in my voice. He sauntered into the living room where I was perusing the catalogue. "How would you like to travel to Binghamton, New York, to listen to dulcimer music and go to music workshops?"

He looked at me as if not fully understanding what a "cranberry gathering" was but was obviously warming to the idea of our taking a trip together. He hopped onto my lap and rabbit-kicked the catalogue onto the floor with his hind legs as if to fully acquire my attention. He snuggled up to me, putting his paws on my chest, purring.

"We'll need to register and get a motel nearby. And this time, you won't have to stay in the bathroom." He looked up at me as if to say, You have that right, Toots. Not in the motel either. "You can be with me at the gathering for all to admire you. You'd like that, wouldn't you?" I swear that at this moment he opened his mouth, lifted his whiskers, closed his eyes, and gave me a truly human-like smile. There is nothing in this world so soul uplifting and inspiring as a full-blown cat smile directed at you ... nothing.

The Cranberry Dulcimer Gathering began in the 1970s as a monthly gathering at The Cranberry Coffee House at the Universalist-Unitarian Church on Riverside Drive, in Binghamton. It was when hammered dulcimer players John Kleske, Ben Stone, and Bob Wey decided to hold a weekend "hammered dulcimer party" for playing and sharing. It would be for hammered dulcimers and Appalachian dulcimers. It was Bob Wey, a very talented musician (winning the National Hammered Dulcimer Championship in 1977), teacher, and engineer, who became the general manager of the event. He did not want it to take on the philosophical cloak of a "festival." Instead, he envisioned it as a casual coming together of that musical community. Initially there were no workshops but they developed over time.

Binghamton seemed a particularly good northeastern location because it was at the crossroads of interstates from all directions of the compass. It was over the northern border of Pennsylvania, south of Syracuse, south west of Albany, east of New England, and accessible from anywhere in New York State. There was no registration or admission fee, though a small donation was requested to cover the printing and mailing expenses incurred by Andy's Front Hall.

A month before the Cranberry Gathering, on June 22, Faust and I celebrated the anniversary of his adoption at the Goodnow Library. For it I had purchased a small can of salmon, piled a tablespoon of it on some greens on his plate, put on a small birthday candle which I lighted. He looked uncomfortably at the flame so I extinguished it quickly. After his meal, I presented him with a two-inch pot, decorated with a red ribbon. It contained a small catnip plant in full leaf. He sniffed, punctured a leaf with his fangs, tore it off, and jumped to the floor before he fell on his head in his narcotics-induced wild cat abandon. I said, "Happy Anniversary, Faust." But he didn't hear me. He was already hugging the pot with his front and back legs, ravenously ravishing the plant in his psychotropic ecstasy.

In late July I made a reservation at a Best Western on the eastern edge of Binghamton. I packed the car for the weekend and we left around noon on Friday. As we left home, Faust was bouncing with enthusiasm, leaping into the backseat with our luggage and supplies, then back onto my lap to stare out the side window. I wasn't sure if it was just because we were going someplace new or he sensed this was going to be a special adventure.

The three hundred and five-mile trip took us over five hours, driving west on the Massachusetts Turnpike to Springfield, then turning north by northwest to Albany and Syracuse then southwest to Binghamton. Binghamton is scenically located in the Appalachian Mountains which were beautiful when the season changed and all the hardwoods began to turn red, orange, pink, and lavender.

At our motel room I carried in our gear and Faust's foldable litter pan with its plastic lining. It took a two-by-four to the back of my head to get me to not bring his large plastic litter pan along. When full of litter, it was too awkward to easily maneuver on and off of the floor of the backseat of the car. Besides it weighed at least fourteen pounds which my back did not appreciate, particularly at that hernia-inducing angle needed to place or remove it.

The coated, foldable, disposable pans were a boon except for the plastic liner. The advertising had urged you to put it in the foldable pan so you could cleanly remove the used litter. That sounded so neat and handy. But it was an absolute disaster. Every paw movement in the litter snagged the plastic, created holes, and pulled it and the litter out of the cardboard pan and onto the car's black floor carpeting.

When we arrived at the church Saturday morning, there was parking on the grass as well as in the paved parking lot and on the street. This event had attracted more people than I had imagined. It was a mob scene. On the lawn outside the backdoor of the church were set up metal folding chairs and hammered dulcimers galore on their slanted wood or metal stands. Two fiddlers and a penny whistle player were gathered together on the far side near a large oak tree, seemingly deciding what reel or jig to play.

A tall, middle-aged male, balding with a longish blond hair and bushy sideburns, was playing a banjo. His female companion, whose long brown hair, parted in the middle, flowed over the shoulders of her ankle-length dress, was plucking an Appalachian dulcimer. I later discovered they were the well-known Rick and Lorraine

Lee. She later came to be called the "Godmother" of mountain dulcimers.

A young, slim blond man, named Rick Fogel, was sharing music theory and the physics of the hammered dulcimer, which he had put into a six-dollar booklet he made available. He said he had composed it while living in a tent for the winter at Point Couverden on the Icy Strait in Alaska. It was becoming obvious that those present were people who enjoyed doing lots of different things ... not constrained to your "everyday suburban life" as I knew it. The atmosphere was one of fun, excitement, and camaraderie. I couldn't wait to see what the program would hold.

Grabbing a chair, I settled in. Faust, in his harness with his leash in my hand, however, decided to start underneath the chair. He seemed to want to get the lay of the land before sharing himself with all those assembled. Bob Wey got everyone's attention to explain the locations of the food, which had been donated, and the restrooms, when the lunch break would occur, where we were invited to eat, in the church recreation room or outside, and how the program would go.

There were workshops of all kinds but what appealed to me were the ones on the basics of hammered dulcimer, different styles of playing for the more advanced student, and music theory. Moreover, there were all kinds of tempting musical merchandise available inside for purchase. You could speak with players and makers during the lunch break. The cliché about being like a kid in a candy store was never more à propos. It felt like being in a musical fantasyland or an invited guest at Julliard Music School who could tour and listen to anything and everything at will.

It wasn't long before Faust came out from under the chair to let everyone know of his presence. Bob Wey, who was walking by, was one of the first to talk to him. As it turned out Bob and his wife were long-time cat aficionados ("ailurophiles," he reminded me) and human companions to several cats. Faust apparently could tell Bob was a kindred spirit. He stood up on his hind legs to rub his face against Bob's legs, delighting Bob.

With Faust's introduction to the cranberry gathering being so favorable, he leapt onto my lap to get the attention of other attendees as well. Bob began to enthusiastically point him out as others also spotted him on their own. Faust was quickly becoming the non-musical star of the weekend. People covered him with oohs and ahhs, and hands grappled to stroke him.

When Bill Spence played some dance tunes, Faust rose to his feet and did his own short version of a jig without my prompting. I was so wrapped up in Spence's playing that I almost missed Faust's performance. Fortunately some seated near me didn't.

"I've never seen that before. A cat who dances? Does he dance like that all the time? How did you get him to do that?"

I almost felt embarrassed to have to admit I couldn't take credit for his terpsichorean talents. I managed to utter with a humble smile, "He's self-taught."

"Oh, wow! Hey, Charley, look at this cat. You've got to see this cat! He dances."

Intermittently throughout the day Faust tripped the light fantastic on the grass. I had the impression that the music inspired him to move, rather than he was trying to get more attention. He knew he didn't have to do anything to get attention. Every time someone wandered by, he received petting, awed responses, and appreciative questions.

The spread for lunch was enormous but a little less so for vegetarians. I purchased a tuna salad which Faust and I shared. Of course, with him sitting on his chair, daintily eating his portion, he garnered more comments and praise. There was no question Faust was going to be impossible to live with after all this.

When we had finished lunch, he had some water and a trip outside the playing and seating areas to relieve himself. Back in the rec hall, we looked at all the varied musical instruments on display I was dying to closely inspect. There were hammered dulcimers, recorders, penny whistles, banjos, fiddles, ocarinas, and Appalachian dulcimers. There was even an autoharp, as well as strings, tuning wrenches, tuners, hammers of fancy designs and exotic woods, and picks for any and all stringed instruments. Faust was settled in on my shoulders. While I was looking, he was being continually petted from behind as attendees passed by us.

There were three different hammered dulcimers that I tentatively banged on with their wooden mallets as I talked to the maker. One was from a kit I could purchase. One was what the maker had made as his general all-round instrument for sale. And one was made exclusively for a purchaser, to his or her particular specifications. It had engraved decorations in its sound holes on its ebony soundboard and special wood and mother of pearl inlays. As I spoke with the maker about construction and price, Faust seemed to be getting restless. He kept changing position. I made the mistake of ignoring him.

Suddenly, he leapt from my shoulders. He landed on the soundboard of the kit-made dulcimer. He tried to paw the taut strings only to discover he had to be careful they didn't cut into the skin between his toes. Time stood still. My heart stopped. I knew I was going into cardiac arrest ... right there on the pale blue linoleum floor. It was only a second before I grabbed him, but it seemed like an eternity. In that second's time, however, he had actually played a few notes. And before I raised his body totally off the instrument, he had played a few more. When I bought a hammered dulcimer, he was going to try to play that too. Oh, good. I couldn't wait. I could picture him lounging on it, loosening the strings

My face was red in my extreme embarrassment. I was gasping for breath. Fear that I might have to purchase that instrument because Faust had done something irreparable to it reared its ugly head in my thoughts. With him safely under my arm, I couldn't stop apologizing. It was as if I were caught in my own continuous babbling loop which was beginning to embarrass the maker. He repeatedly assured me the instrument was fine. He showed me the strings. They were still taut and in place. The sound was still fine.

I smiled at the maker, took his card, murmured, "Thanks a lot, Faust," under my breath, and slunk away. The maker called after me, "Maybe your cat would like a few lessons while he's here." I waved in recognition that he had said something terribly droll but kept moving. The musical evening joyfully seemed to go on forever.

But I had to leave. I hated to but I was tired.

The next morning, with the car re-packed after checking out of the motel, we headed back to the once-again mobbed church to attend the basic hammered dulcimer workshop. We listened to the various scheduled performers, including Bob Wey, Jim Cousa and Maddie McNeil, and caught jam sessions on the side. Bob Wey, who was from Westford, Massachusetts, joined us a couple to times to ask if we had heard about some other Massachusetts events. One was the Flower Carol Dulcimer Festival in Watertown and the other was New England Folk Festival (NEFFA) in Natick. The Flower Carol attracted a wide range of instruments and workshops from Appalachian dulcimer to lute to banjo to fiddle to hammered dulcimer to harpsichord to Celtic harp. And NEFFA added to that Morris dancing and folk dancing, singing, and anything even remotely related to early and current folk music.

I put them on my list of travel destinations along with my long-held plans to finally visit the national parks ... now with Faust. This informal gathering had truly inspired me. I wanted more, lots more. Every time I was introduced to a new and wonderful musical instrument, I could picture having it in my home and playing it as well. My fantasy list was growing: penny whistle, recorder, and Celtic harp in addition to the hammered dulcimer, of course. And maybe once I learned to play at least one of them—the hammered dulcimer would have to be first—I could join a group and jam with it. Making music together could add so much to my life. Of course, I'd have to bring Faust along to enjoy it as well.

Musicians were still going strong as Faust and I readied to leave for home. Numbers of hammered dulcimer players were playing the traditional Irish reel, "Swinging on the Gate" with all kinds of flourishes. It sounded great. A banjo and several fiddles joined in. There was a group of penny whistlers who picked up the tune as well. It sounded so sprightly that your feet couldn't stop tapping or dancing. Faust was on the ground, giving it his all, unwilling to leave.

But with five hours to go, I wanted to start before it got dark. Once again I hated to be one of the first to go. Everyone was having so much fun. And I wanted to continue to have it along with them for as long as possible. Before we finally settled ourselves in the car, I had made a point of saying good-bye to everyone we had met. I especially wanted to keep in contact with Bob Wey. We were weary with our ears still ringing with the sounds of every conceivable type of music played on the hammered dulcimer ... and every other type of instrument. Others playing music was caressing my heart. But my listening to it was caressing my soul. We had lapped up Christmas carols, Bach, Elizabethan dances, Appalachian classics, and Celtic traditional tunes, including pieces by 17th-18th Century blind Irish harper, composer, Turlough O'Carolan, as if we were dining on cream.

Whoever still had a camera handy happily snapped their last-minute pictures of Faust as he posed for them. I was in the photos too ... well, only if you counted my fingers, hand, or arm happening to be in their field of view some place near him. Some even promised to send me copies, but never did. I thought it was a long shot that we'd receive them with so much going on.

Again I hadn't brought my camera because I didn't want to try to juggle Faust, my handbag, food, a camera, or anything else I might purchase, such as music cassettes and thirty-three and a third albums. So regretfully I had no photos of him in Binghamton. I definitely would have to figure out a way to accommodate a camera too next time—whether at the next Cranberry Gathering, Flower Carol, or NEFFA. There was no question that we absolutely had to have a camera when we went on our trek to the national parks. I was promising us both. We both needed pictures to look at, smile and sigh over, and rekindle the fond memories of our excursions together. Faust made every trip an adventure I wouldn't forget soon.

CHAPTER 22

NAVIGATING HOME
✳✳

The trip back started out fine with Faust cat-napping on my lap. Then he decided to transfer to my shoulders so he could look out occasionally to see if there was anything of interest ... like birds flying over. The sky had spun from a Baroque blue to cotton candy pink which, in turn, silently slipped on kitty paws into lavender. On the horizon the hot red sun was being diluted by gold, shifting to apricot then settling into yellow. As we made our way through the increasing darkness, I found that I was feeling really tired. I hadn't slept all that well at the motel so I figured I'd better stop at a gas station restaurant outside Albany for coffee.

When I returned to the car, Styrofoam cup in hand, Faust crawled back around my neck. I found I had to stop again for another cup. But by the time we reached the Massachusetts Turnpike, I found I needed something a lot stronger: caffeine tablets, amphetamine, a bucket of ice poured down my back—anything to keep my eyelids from drooping.

I had already begun to instantly disappear from consciousness. Hour-like seconds passed until something woke me. So far I was staying in the right lane, but I wasn't sure how much longer I could manage to do that. I turned on the radio and started loudly singing with whatever was on whether I knew the lyrics or melody or not. Suddenly I was veering off the road. I barely caught myself as I crossed the white line at the right-hand edge, nearly throwing a glancing blow at the guard rail.

Opening the driver's side window a little, I let the cool air caress my face. That wasn't enough. I couldn't keep my eyes open. I stuck my face out the window to let the wind slap me. But that wasn't enough either. Next I turned on the air-conditioner full blast. This only made me shiver along my back, leaving my eyelids untouched. Feeling desperate, I turned it off again. What to do? Nothing was helping. Faust stirred slightly and I kept dozing off. Hypnotized by the never-ending broken white line in the center of the road in the darkness, I faded out until something woke me. I felt dead to the world, incapable of reviving myself.

It seemed incredible that the fear that gripped my heart now wasn't enough to shake my torpor. It was like I had taken sleeping pills or too much antihistamine. Next I tried dancing in my seat. I hopped up and down to the music on the radio. I shoved my left foot against the floor boards, vigorously tapping to keep rhythm. It helped ... but only for a minute.

I faded out again. This time I veered out of the right lane, nearly into the heavy growth of maples and oak trees. Suddenly awake again, I screamed out loud, "I'm going to get us killed!" What was I going to do? I was trying everything that experts suggested when sleepiness had overwhelmed you. And not a damned thing was working. I was becoming frantic.

If being scared of driving off the road was not enough to awaken me, would anything? I was at my wit's end. I needed to pull over for a nap. We were on a long stretch of wooded nothingness. There was no way it could be safe. We could be hit by another sleepy driver ... or ... well, something worse. But my driving wasn't safe either. Thinking a little *real* exercise might help, I checked for traffic in the lanes behind me—there was none—and pulled over any way. I moved as far to the right as I could without scraping the intermittent guard rail.

Unwrapping Faust from my neck, I exited the car. Breathing deeply, I jogged back and forth in front of the car eight times. I did some pathetic pushups. My heart was pounding. Adrenaline was racing to my limbs. I was sure this was going to work. But, as impossible as it seemed, the adrenaline wasn't reaching my eyelids. They were just as leaden as before, wanting to close and stay closed.

Faust looked around to see if we were home yet. Standing at the open driver's side door, still breathing hard, I murmured, "Faust, everything is okay. We'll be home soon." But would we—would we really? I was scared we wouldn't make it, becoming road kill ... or worse. I climbed back into the car. Faust re-wrapped himself around my neck. Vowing we would spend as much time as I needed at the next rest stop—assuming there was one coming up some place—I plunged again into the night's blackness, feeling disoriented, hoping for the best.

Each time we veered off to the right something woke me just in time to get us back on the road before we crashed. I had no idea how that happened. My brain felt too heavy and fuzzy to figure it out. I knew I couldn't depend on something continuing to wake me up *just in time*. A green highway sign with fluorescent lettering seemed to pop up out of nowhere. It announced a rest area a mile up ahead. Thank goodness. If only we can make it there.

Somehow we did make it, though I don't know how. I pulled in. Without looking around at the entire parking lot, I stopped and incautiously raced to the women's restroom area. After relieving myself, I spent a few minutes at the sink, repeatedly splashing and slapping my face with cold water. With a hint of consciousness, it occurred to me that my coming into this building all alone had been a risky move. I had no idea who might be lurking here, thief or rapist, waiting for some unsuspecting woman to appear. But I had no choice. "Damned if you do and damned if you don't."

Feeling only momentarily a little more awake, I scanned the lot for a place to park so I could sleep. Of course, I knew sleeping would likewise be risky, even with the doors locked and windows up. But at the moment I would have given almost anything to lie in the arms or Morpheus for even a little while.

It was only then that I noticed the parking lot was vacant except for a lone black sedan. It was to the left of the ladies' room where I stood. In it sat two men. I couldn't see their faces clearly but they seemed to be watching me from the driver's side window. Uneasiness squeezed my heart. Purposely I strode military-fashion back to my car. I hoped that would show them I was no fragile flower but one who probably knew karate and had the confidence to use it. Once inside I decided to wait to see if they would leave.

Minutes passed as I tried to keep my eyes open. It seemed to be a useless endeavor. My head kept falling backward then snapping forward again. I glanced their way. They didn't seem to be readying to go. Despite wanting to sleep more than I ever had before, I waited some more. Still there was no movement from them or their car. Maybe they were having the same problem as I and were there to take a nap too. But their actions didn't correspond with that hope. They didn't seem to be relaxing. Instead, they kept looking our way. What little confidence I had at that moment was rapidly seeping out of me

After twenty minutes of struggling to stay awake, I decided we couldn't stay there any longer, despite my lustful desire to snooze. There were no cars coming into the rest stop which could help if it were needed. I had no weapon. And while Faust was, I'm sure, a cat to be reckoned with, he was no match for two men if it came to that.

"I'm sorry, Faust," I whispered to him, rubbing my warm, dry cheek against his face. "It looks as though we're going to have to take our chances on the road." The idea of putting his life at risk gave me pause. I gave them a few more minutes. They didn't move. What were they doing? They just sat there, continuing to look in my direction. It had already begun to feel creepy, like an episode from the "Twilight Zone" or "Tales From the Dark Side." Then my heart sank. The moment I turned on my engine, they turned on theirs. Fear clutched my gut. My heart was pounding in my ears. My intestines turned to liquid.

As I put the car in gear and started to pull out, they did likewise. Now they were behind me, following me. Somehow the adrenaline had finally made its way to my eyelids. They were no longer at half-mast. Now I was fully focused on the road ... and on their car. What were they doing? Why were they doing this? I still couldn't see their faces through their windshield even when we passed under the bright overhead highway lights. This was no co-incidence. They had some kind of plan in mind. Were they going to try to run me off the road and —? Were they going to follow me home? I was a lone female in the dark in the boonies in a car that was not known for its Grand Prix competition status. At least I wasn't in a Beetle.

They followed two car-lengths behind. When I sped up, they sped up. When I slowed down, they slowed down. Visions of abduction, rape, and murder were dancing in front of me. I was suddenly reminded of Richard Matheson's frightening story, "Duel," which was made into a movie starring Dennis Weaver. In it a semi-truck tailgates Weaver's car for miles and miles and tries to kill him by running him into a train or off the road. If these two were trying to scare the bejeezus of out me, they were doing a smash up job. If only I had a car phone. If only there were an emergency phone at the side of the road. Well, crap, even if there were an emergency phone, there was no way I could get to it *without* stopping and getting out of the car. What was someone in the hinterlands on a state highway supposed to do to get help?

Since we had left the rest stop, I had searched for a state police car. Nothing was parked along the way. Nothing passed to which I could attempt to signal my distress. Not a state trooper for miles and miles and miles. Didn't they patrol the Mass. Pike? I looked for other traffic and there was none. Nothing was ahead or behind us. What the hell? I considered pulling off at some—any—exit to search for a police station. But there was no guaranteed I'd find one. I still had no idea where I was. What if I got caught on a dead end street or just got lost? I would really be at their mercy. It felt safer to stay on the turnpike where I could try to out-run or out-maneuver them. I had no idea what speed my standard-shift Rabbit could potentially achieve, but at least it could turn on a dime.

My heart was leaping out of my chest as I constantly checked my rear view mirror. I couldn't see their license plate. I still couldn't see them. They were right there on my tail. What were they going to do next? I could hardly swallow for lack of saliva. What could *I* do? All that occurred to me was to continue to drive ... and hope for the best. As I moved to the left lane, they followed. As I moved back right, they did the same. They never tried to come up beside me or pass me. They were like a gangrenous appendix for the last twenty miles.

Then to my shock, the sedan suddenly pulled off at the exit I had just passed. I was in a state of suspended emotion. They had followed me trying to intimidate me, and had royally succeeded. All my fear and rage screamed for expression. I shouted at the top of my lungs, "You bastards! You sons of bitches! You did that purposely to frighten me! That was too cruel for words! I hope you rot in hell ... hanging up by your testicles." I wanted to cry until I had no tears left but I felt too dry and spent to cry.

I had a throbbing headache. My shoulders, neck, and arms ached from the strain. My calves were cramping. I didn't understand how they could have done that. If they could do that to me, what could they ... and did they ... do to others who were likewise vulnerable. I looked at Faust with his eyes closed. I didn't want to think about it any longer. He was safe and that was what was important. As far as I knew, so was I. The rest of the way to Sudbury I kept my eyes wide open and the car on the road.

When we arrived home, it was just before midnight. Faust enthusiastically jumped off my shoulders and out of the car. I dragged myself in behind him. Looking at all that needed to be brought inside from the car, I said aloud, "Forget it. I'll do it in the morning." I brushed my teeth, after having debated whether to bother. Looking in the mirror at the many scratches on my left cheek, I vaguely wondered where they came from. But at that moment, I didn't really care. Giving Faust his nightly snack and some fresh water, I checked all the doors, windows, rooms, and closets. Then I trudged into the bedroom, stripped off my outerwear, and slipped on my man's tall tee-shirt. I took the baseball bat out of the closet and put it under my pillow, against the headboard.

As I crawled into bed, I was never happier to be home. Faust likewise had checked out the house for me. When he was satisfied everything was as it should be, that nothing had been disturbed in our absence, that there were no strange smells, he crawled onto my chest. As I was falling asleep on my back, he snuggled under my chin. He placed his paws around my neck, and stretched his body out the length of my upper torso. He started his muffler-less purr. Then he licked the scratches on my cheek as if to say, Everything is okay now. I love you, Mom. Where are we going next?

I didn't tell him but we'd soon be heading cross-country to see some of the exquisite natural wonders of America.

CHAPTER 23

WHAT FAUST TAUGHT ME

✷✷

For the fourteen years I had been without Sam, I experienced a loss that left a deep, wide hole in my life ... in my heart. Having a cat companion had been an integral part of my life. When Faust arrived, I finally put Sam and the loss of his companionship into perspective and into the past. I could see how much that bond had meant to me and how much I really truly missed it.

Faust gave me another chance to intimately know and enjoy another cat's unique personality, antics, and love. His having been homeless when I rescued him added another important dimension to our relationship. Homeless animals have suffered emotionally and physically and are so grateful for love and care. Altogether, he gave new meaning to my life ... as I did to his.

I have discovered that I have become a much better person for having had him as my companion. I am more open, welcoming, and sharing. I listen more carefully and patiently. I am more aware of nonverbal behaviors and hold off on making assumptions.

I don't need to tap into research to know that having a cat companion is exceedingly therapeutic for anyone. But it is especially true for those who are alone, stressed, anxious, depressed, grieving, or ill. It can positively improve your emotional state, by alleviating your stress, and your health, by lowering your blood pressure. Whenever I was down, Faust could perk me up. Whenever I was ill, he snuggled up and kept me warm and comforted. Reflecting a sympathetic resonance, he gave me the chance to nurture and feel needed. Interacting with Faust gave me someone to care for and about—someone who cared for and about me back.

My relationship with Faust also influenced me directly in social situations. People with animals are thought to be friendlier, happier, more caring, more hardworking, and intelligent so others approach us more positively and frequently. When I was walking with him, I experienced exceedingly more social contact and longer conversations than when I was walking alone. I found this repeatedly.

Faust attracted other people like a powerful electro-magnet. He gave them an easy and casual, ever-ready topic to happily discuss even with a stranger. You could talk about a cat walking with a harness, training for cats, cat shows, but especially about their own experiences with a cat as a pet or just in passing. He always elicited a smile from people—whether by his dancing, willingness to touch and be touched, or his vampire teeth—seeming to make them happy they had encountered him.

Furthermore, his presence always required me to rise to the occasion. I would meet new people, communicate with them, and become more comfortable and confident in doing so. He made me feel good about myself as a result. I felt I belonged to a wider, caring community.

I have had a cherished relationship with Faust. He has enriched my life by:

- Being non-judgmental
- Never criticizing me
- Always being open
- Accepting me even when I've made mistakes or had done stupid things
- Encouraging me to share anything and everything with him without fear of embarrassment
- Demonstrating sincere affection
- Listening attentively and empathetically to me
- Making me more attentive to body language and its interpretations
- Greeting me with an ever-ready smile
- Sensing my feelings and being there for me

What Faust the Dancing Cat Taught Me

- Distracting me when I needed it
- Touching me and savoring my touch in return
- Demonstrating his trust in me
- Being honest and forthright—never lying to me
- Never betraying me
- Having no hidden agendas
- Teaching me patience and persistence
- Making me aware of time-pressuring myself
- Showing me how to play, have fun, and relax
- Allowing me to rely on him to be there
- Providing a consistent and permanent relationship
- Showing me how to truly listen to another being—cat or human
- Remaining my loyal friend
- Being my enthusiastic playmate
- Helping me to stop jumping to conclusions
- Helping me step outside my assumptions and beliefs about what cats and people can do.

I now fully recognize what a rare opportunity it has been to share my life with a cat companion. Faust has impacted me physically, emotionally, psychically, and spiritually. Furthermore, he has met many of my emotional and psychological needs that humans often simply can't meet because of their own issues and self-involvement.

We humans like to think—maybe even pride ourselves—that we are so much more complex than cats. That may be true in some respects. But I think that what we really pride ourselves on being is multi-taskers, taking everything super-seriously, and just being more harried as a result. Faust has taught me we don't have to be. In fact, we can choose not to be. We can become more mindful of what really matters—love and relationships—and less time-obsessed so we can smell the flowers (or the catnip leaves). But most of all he has shown me what unending unconditional love and acceptance are. And he has graciously given them to me. Thank you, Faust, for this. And this was only the start of our wild-and-woolly adventures together.

ABOUT THE AUTHOR

Signe A. Dayhoff, PhD, MA, MEd, is a social psychologist from Boston University with post-graduate training in counseling, emotional intelligence, and positive psychology. For over 30 years she has been a cognitive-behaviorist, coach, educator, and author, specializing in increasing interpersonal communication and self-confidence and alleviating social anxiety. An applied feline behaviorist and rescuer, she is kitty-mom to 20-plus senior cats and consults on improving human-cat relationships and creating human-cat communication.

She has taught psychology at Boston University, University of Massachusetts, and Framingham State College and has done research at Massachusetts Institute of Technology, Scripps Clinic and Research Foundation, and Fairview State Hospital.

She is author of seventeen books: *Attracting and Dating the Wrong Men: Tips and Insights to Free Yourself; Growing Up "Unacceptable"—How Katharine Hepburn Rescued Me; How Insiders Get Jobs: 6-Mini-Course Series; Scared of Your Boss? Smash Through Your Fear Now; Promote Myself? I'd Rather Eat Worms!; How to Speak Without Fear Small Talk Course*; 2nd Ed. of

Diagonally-Parked in a Parallel Universe: Working Through Social Anxiety); *Create Your Own Career Opportunities; Get The Job You Want;* and *Decision Making For Managers.* And she contributed to David Riklan's *101 Great Ways to Improve Your Life (Vol. 2)* and Steven J. Bennett's *Executive Chess: Creative Problem Solving By 45 of America's Top Business Leaders and Thinkers.*